PORTRAITS OF
Success

9 KEYS TO SUSTAINING VALUE IN ANY BUSINESS

James Olan Hutcheson

Dearborn™
Trade Publishing
A **Kaplan Professional** Company

This publication is designed to provide accurate and authoritative information in regard to the subject matter covered. It is sold with the understanding that the publisher is not engaged in rendering legal, accounting, or other professional service. If legal advice or other expert assistance is required, the services of a competent professional should be sought.

The information about the people and organizations described in this book was gathered from the author's personal experiences; from family members and employees of Olan Mills, Inc.; from books, articles, and published reports, including official company documents; and from interviews conducted by the author's research staff. To protect the privacy of clients and other people, the identities of some of the companies and executives have been concealed by altering names, locations, and other identifying details.

Vice President and Publisher: Cynthia A. Zigmund
Editorial Director: Donald J. Hull
Acquisitions Editor: Mary B. Good
Senior Project Editor: Trey Thoelcke
Interior Design: Lucy Jenkins
Cover Design: Design Solutions
Typesetting: Elizabeth Pitts

© 2002 by Dearborn Financial Publishing, Inc.

Published by Dearborn Trade Publishing, a Kaplan Professional Company

Printed in the United States of America

02 03 04 10 9 8 7 6 5 4 3 2 1

Library of Congress Cataloging-in-Publication Data

Hutcheson, James Olan.
    Portraits of success : 9 keys to sustaining value in any business / James Olan Hutcheson.
        p.   cm.
Includes index.
    ISBN 0-7931-5259-3
    1. Family-owned business enterprises—United States—Management. 2. Close corporations—United States—Management. 3. Success in business—United States. 4. Businesspeople—United States—Attitudes. 5. Successful people—United States.   I. Title.
    HD62.25 .H88 2002
    658'.045—dc21

                                                                            2002003513

Dearborn Trade books are available at special quantity discounts to use for sales promotions, employee premiums, or educational purposes. Please call our special sales department, to order or for more information, at 800-621-9621, ext. 4307.

IN HONOR OF

My grandfathers, Olan Mills and Lewis "Dutch" Hutcheson
My grandmother, Jean Hutcheson
My brother, Travis T. Hutcheson
My sensei, Master Robert A. Trias

CONTENTS

ACKNOWLEDGMENTS vii

PREFACE
My Business Story xi
Olan Mills, Inc. xviii

INTRODUCTION
Building Companies That Last 1
Legend Airlines 11

CHAPTER 1
The Secret of Great Business Leadership 21
Richard Wackenhut 37

CHAPTER 2
Make It a Meritocracy 48
Dennis Rodman 59

CHAPTER 3
Give the Next Generation Room to Grow 65
Carr Tilton 68
Robert Dedman, Jr. 73
Katz's Deli 78

CHAPTER 4
Finding a Common Direction 81
George Steinbrenner 86
Dell and Compaq 99

CHAPTER 5
Make Communication Central 102
Warren Buffett 115
Newell Farms 130

CHAPTER 6
The Journey of Passion and Balance 134
Williamson-Dickie 135
J. Paul Getty 148
Jon Huntsman 159

CHAPTER 7
Create Business Traditions, Myths, and Shared Beliefs 164
Herbert Kelleher 165
Teresa Lever-Pollary 169

CHAPTER 8
Do the Strongest Really Survive? 184
Stora Enso 185
"Chainsaw" Al Dunlap 192

CHAPTER 9
Managing Risk 199
Robert Uihlein 203
Fred Smith 205
Gene Amdahl 212

CONCLUSION
Closing Reflections 215

INDEX 223

ACKNOWLEDGMENTS

You are holding the end result of a project that stirred in me for several years. I had often thought about what it would be like to write a book, but thinking and doing proved to be entirely different experiences. Paraphrasing Churchill, writing a book is an adventure—starting as an amusement, turning into a mistress, a master, and ending as a tyrant that rules your life. After completing *Portraits of Success*, I can truthfully admit that my fondness for Churchill's insight has grown even deeper.

I was able to escape the maws of the tyrant only with the aid of many others who, at just the right time, jumped in and gave me strength and encouragement to press onward. I can recall few experiences or projects in my life where my debts, and learning, have risen faster. Although the words and concepts are mine, this book is not mine alone. So many people have been a part of its development and influenced me that it is inappropriate to not recognize those who helped shape my thinking, gave me support, provided friendship and love, and fought for my cause.

This book would never have moved out of the amusement stage if it were not for the day in day out help from my ReGENERATION Partners colleagues, Debra Krueger and Jerry McNabb.

Thanks to Tom Wilkinson, Nancy Lynn, Nancy Blackie, and Jo Ann Alvarez, all of whom worked with me at Olan Mills, Inc. Their service and loyalty is never taken for granted. Additionally, I received help from many of my predecessors at Olan Mills who took the time to pass and entrust the stories of my grandfather to me. Thank you Tom Roberts, Ray Zbinden, Fred Tregaskis, Ollie Collie, Ruth Clark, Jane Glass, Bonnie Williams, Bill Taylor, and Olan Mills II.

Making the wholesale change from a corporate executive to a full-time family business consultant was, at times, difficult. Thank you to all of those who not only believed in me but also helped in tangible ways, especially the three Davids—David Bork, David Clanton, and David Waring.

I am indebted to some pros who with one hand held mine, and with the other furiously maneuvered the editing pencil. Thank you Mark Henricks, Ron Watkins, Dennis Jaffe, Ph.D., and Mary B. Good. Among this illustrious group, more than 37 books have been authored or coauthored. It is a good thing to have a few talented professionals as close friends.

Speaking of friends, one of the greatest joys of my adult life has been to share the ups and downs with people I call my close friends. I am blessed to have the laughter, competition, companionship, adventure, and unconditional support from Charles Wait, Ed Elkins, Tom Box, Joe Best, Greg Baten, Greg Rohde, Gary Meyer, and, of course, Mike Cofield, Ph.D., whom I have considered family, friend, and mentor for over 35 years.

This book would not have been possible without the added learning that has come from clients of ReGENERATION Partners. These are the people who trusted us with their family businesses and provided the real stories and anecdotes that have enriched the message of this book. Thank you, Nicki, for being one of our first.

And special thanks to Stan Baxter, Gerry Sullivan, and Jeff Sullivan, clients whose enthusiasm for this project, at times, exceeded my own. Their perspective as business owners and CEOs provided the truest test of relevance. I can attest that it is true that you gain more in life by helping others.

Ordinary people with an extraordinary message have come into my life at just the right moments to assume the mantle of mentor. Their messages have helped to form my core values. Thank you Stanley Albert "Buck" Frame, Don Benton, Jay Ekman, Vann Phillips, and Master Robert A. Trias.

The tasks of this book and so many other projects in life would not have been conceivable without the support and patience of a caring family. Thank you to Carole Lou, Lewis, Laura, and Henry. Thanks to all the Warrens, Mills, and Hutchesons that helped shape me into the person I have become. With special thanks to Sharon, the godmother of my children, my aunt, and part-time editor. To Pat and Skip, who at various times have been teachers, best friends, advisors, playmates, and editors, but who have always shared my pains and celebrated my joys as supportive and loving parents.

Those that know me best say I am full of passion for whatever I do in life. This is true. This passion comes from the love and support of a wife who has been traveling through life with me, often at a sprint, for over 20 years. My greatest thanks are for Sarah, serving as a mother, teacher, friend, and wife. She keeps my zest for new adventures alive.

And finally, the greatest source of joy in my life is our two sons, Nathan and Warren. I have been blessed with children who have not only overlooked my absence and made excuses for my exhaustion, but have forced me to keep my priorities straight. Their love and joy gives me strength.

My Business Story

Chances are, you carry photographs of people you love in your wallet or billfold. If you examine these photographs, you will probably discover in the lower right-hand corner of at least one, a gold-embossed representative signature of the man who, in large part, created the portrait photography industry. That man was my grandfather, Olan Mills.

Starting from humble beginnings on a Nebraska farm, Olan Mills swaggered, charmed, blustered, and bullied his way into founding and building the world's premier portrait photography company. At its peak more than 65 years later, Olan Mills, Inc., had more than 1,000 photo studios in the United States, Canada, and the United Kingdom with over 15,000 employees photographing 6.5 million families annually. These numbers enabled Olan Mills, Inc., rightfully to claim the title of *The Nation's Studio*. If you have portraits on display in your home or office, it is largely because of Olan Mills.

Before Olan Mills, photographs were reserved for the privileged. Photographs for all but the well-heeled were taken primarily for record keeping. You've no doubt seen them—grim, unsmiling, foreboding black and whites. Today, we treat these photographs as a novelty. My grandfather saw an opportunity to provide affordable portraits to everyone. Combining his idea of affordable photography with the power of emotions, he began capturing the happiness and expressions of personality on children's faces. He froze in time the joy a young graduate feels while holding their diploma, the pride of a patriot in uniform, and the love parents hold for their families. These photographs marked the passage through life for many children and families, and as they were passed from one generation to the next, became treasured family heirlooms.

Olan Mills, Inc., is my family's business. I worked there for nearly 20 years, beginning humbly as the founder did and working my way up to participate firsthand in key decisions as the business grew and prospered, and faltered and recovered. Since leaving Olan Mills, Inc., as the head of its studio division in 1995, I have been a consultant to a wide variety of other businesses, helping them deal with many of the same issues of leadership, communication, and control that played so big a role at our closely held firm.

This book is my effort to share what I have learned from my perspectives as a long-time senior executive with a prominent and prosperous concern, as an interim CEO with multiple firms, and also as a management consultant working with many different firms. Specifically, I've come to recognize that certain predictable problems afflict closely held businesses, and that successful firms apply and live by certain solutions. These solutions lie in the policies, practices, traditions, values, and strategies that businesses, knowingly or unknowingly, with planning or not, embed within themselves and use in conducting everyday operations.

Leading a firm with the ambition of creating sustainable wealth and success is highly complex. Numerous manuals exist for changing, managing, designing, etc., but few and far between are books about creating sustainable business success. *Portraits of Success* addresses nine vital areas for creating long-term sustainable business success. It deals with such issues as self-esteem—the core character of effective leadership; creating a meritocracy; giving the next generation of leaders room to grow; getting owners, managers, and employees all moving in the same direction; improving communication among leaders; instilling passion and achieving balance; creating a culture rich with business traditions and rituals; building shared beliefs among founders and future management; and how adapting to change and managing risk are accomplished.

The way in which business leaders deal with these key issues determines, in large part, how long and under what circumstances the enterprise will survive. Although I describe nine keys to creating sustainable success, I don't claim this list is all-inclusive. There is no single way to do it right, and there are many more ways to do it wrong.

Still, I start confidently with a sweeping premise: namely, that by recognizing and replicating the solutions and experiences of thriving enterprises, many more firms can enjoy the type of accomplishment that Olan Mills, Inc., experienced for most of its long existence. This book presents Olan Mills, Inc., and the many other firms that I have worked with over the years as a roadmap for readers. By understanding and, where necessary, modifying your beliefs and approach, you can use this roadmap to create a business environment for long-term success.

The first step in creating beliefs, attitudes, and actions that lead to sustainable success is to understand where you have come from and where you are right now. For me the story of Olan Mills, telling how this one company came to be, is an example of what you need to know about your business to implement the keys to business success that follow.

BACK TO THE BEGINNING

Many successful organizations have a story, steeped in tradition, about where and how they came to be. As this book's chapter on building business traditions makes clear, the correlation between stories and traditions, and later success is no coincidence. The Olan Mills story began in the late nineteenth century, when Emma Alberta Terentia and Wyman Morse Mills were born to immigrant farmers from Scotland and Ireland. After their marriage, the two began farming in northern New Jersey. Then, hearing stories of good fortune in the West, they took the advice of Horace Greeley and joined a wagon train.

As the westward movement passed through Nebraska, Wyman and Alberta rooted their dreams in McCook County, not far from the Kansas border. Olan Clarence Mills was born in 1904, the ninth of ten children to arrive at the Mills farm. The family was impoverished by any definition. But the time was filled with optimism and a belief in the Protestant work ethic. Young Olan was exposed to newspapers and dime novels filled with Horatio Alger stories of success that touted America as the land of opportunity. These tales profoundly influenced him.

These images of prosperity had all the more impact in contrast with Olan's hardscrabble upbringing. "Life on the farm was all work and no play," my grandfather would later tell me. As his older brothers and sisters moved off the farm to start their own lives, Olan's childhood became something of an endless chore: tending the chickens, worming the tobacco, and feeding the stock. At 15, in search of a high school education, he left home and traveled to the state capital, Lincoln. With virtually no money, he settled with a wealthy widow who would provide him room and board in exchange for odd jobs around her estate. Among his responsibilities was caring for the garage and maintaining the automobiles. Though the remuneration was modest, this close-up view of a privileged existence had a major impact on the maturing Olan's outlook and objectives as a businessman. It would inspire him for the rest of his life.

In later years, he spoke often of his first employer's opulent and elegant lifestyle. This observation created a deep-rooted desire to achieve material success. As we will see in Chapter 6, not only accomplishing goals but *establishing* goals is a critical component of creating and maintaining a successful business.

Though his means were modest, the ex-farm boy was eager to improve himself and soon enrolled at the nearby University of Nebraska as a premed student. If this sounds brashly ambitious, understand that Olan Mills was, from the beginning, a flamboyant personality, an imaginative self-starter, and a consummate deal maker. College was an opportunity to establish himself as a person of consequence and put some distance between himself and farming, and he tackled it optimistically.

His outgoing and charismatic personality served him well. Always sociable and comfortable in a crowd, he surrounded himself with an eclectic cadre of fraternity brothers, other refugees from rural Nebraska, local merchants, hired help, and, as this was during the Prohibition years, moonshiners. Olan turned out to have a gift for selling as well as a powerful drive to succeed in business. He used his friendships with the university's social clubs and the moonshiners to become a middleman in a bootlegging operation that supplied liquor for fraternity parties.

While the income from his activities funded his studies, unfortunately Olan became a heavy drinker and, eventually, an alcoholic. He would live much of his later years as an alcoholic, creating personal and professional problems for himself and the business. Like many high-achieving businesspeople, Olan's internal personal difficulties were camouflaged and even exacerbated by external success. Later chapters in this book will provide insight to help businesses deal with similar problems. Solutions relate to the need for objective feedback, outside opinions, and self-esteem boosting management practices.

Olan had attended college only a short time when, dissatisfied with opportunities in Nebraska, he followed the land boom into Florida as a traveling salesman—a real-life Charlie Babbitt. The Florida boom was short lived. When rumors of another boom in

xvi PORTRAITS OF SUCCESS

Muscle Shoals, Alabama, reached him, he was on the road again, hitchhiking his way into the neighboring state. When he learned he had missed the boom there as well, he joined a door-to-door crew selling photographic restoration work. This service repaired damaged or faded photos for the families lucky enough to own such mementos.

Characteristically, after a while Olan decided he could sell restoration work just as well on his own as he could with his employer. He set out on his own, traveling through Alabama and knocking on doors in the time-honored manner. His personal approach, however, was a little different from most peddlers of the era. Unlike the typical dusty and travel-worn drummer, he dressed impeccably, in a style usually reserved for movie stars and other celebrities. When he knocked on a door or walked into a room, he was a showstopper. People might not know who he was, but they were pretty sure he was somebody important. He relished the role and, in no small measure, built his company so he could live it.

His travels eventually led him to the town of Selma, Alabama. Many years later, Selma would become famous as the birthplace of the civil rights movement, but at the time it was just another unknown crossroads. It proved significant for Olan, however, for there he found Mary Eula Stephenson, a violinist with the symphony and an accomplished artist. Mary used her artistic training to produce oil paintings of Alabama society, add color to black and white photographs, and perform restoration work on old, cracked, or partially destroyed photographs. When Olan and Mary's paths crossed professionally, Olan was smitten with the young artist's renowned beauty and red hair, described by Tom Roberts, the company's first employee and a boarder in the Mills household, as "the color of a baked sweet potato with a pat of melted butter." She was impressed with his high-toned appearance and dynamism.

After a brief courtship, Olan and Mary were wed in 1929. The first two of the couple's four children were born in quick succession: Patricia Marie, my mother, was the second child. With Mary's parents, the family shared a small home on a dirt street. The house was full of artist's supplies, and piles of worn photographs were everywhere. Mary's two small children were constantly on the go while her husband, dressed as an ambassador, came and went with orders for restoration work. It was a busy, tumultuous, close-pressed existence. This type of togetherness, with people in close contact and communication, is important for creating and maintaining the kind of shared vision that keeps companies healthy. It will be discussed in later chapters on conducting meetings, finding a common direction, and building shared beliefs.

Life was, however, difficult. This was during the Depression, in a small town where wealth was scarce. Realizing Selma offered a limited future and still clinging to his aspirations, Olan decided to move the family to Tuscaloosa, the nearby hub of central Alabama, where they rented a room in a decaying boarding house.

Even though the family was still financially strapped, to keep Mary working at her easel, a servant named Margaret was hired to care for and help raise the babies. Margaret became the glue that held the family together. She remained a focus of love and admiration for all the Mills children, the early employees of Olan Mills, and, to some extent, the grandchildren during her 101 years. She was a very special person who probably never realized how much she touched the Mills children. Even today, my mother in all earnestness states, "Margaret raised me. She was always there for us." Many firms have discovered the value of long-time employees but are not sure how to nurture it. Chapters in this book on honest feedback and impartial mentoring will explain why, and how, you can get similar benefits for your firm.

Tuscaloosa provided new hope for Olan and Mary's new business. As with many openings, it sprang from an obstacle. Most people at that time lived on farms or in small towns and had limited access to luxuries such as personal cameras and professional photography studios. As he traveled across Alabama selling restoration services, Olan observed that many families had no need for restoration services because they simply had no photos to begin with. But he was sure that parents desired photos of their children, especially those grown children serving in the U.S. military in far away lands. He recognized an opportunity.

PORTRAIT OF SUCCESS

Olan Mills, Inc.

During the Depression, a college dropout peddled wares in and around the streets of Selma, Alabama. By most accounts his method was in the tradition of a P.T. Barnum. He was a promoter, a cocksure salesman.

Seeing no future in odd jobs, the young salesman set out to capitalize on a relatively new invention—the camera. When most American families could not afford the high cost of a portrait artist or professional photographer, the young man proposed to sell affordable photographic portraits to families with children.

He began without investors and with virtually no capital. He borrowed a camera from a neighbor. Initially, the young man could not afford to buy the one necessary supply—film. Such obstacles, however, were slight in the eyes of a man who held passion and conviction for his plans.

An inveterate problem solver, the young man adopted a creative strategy to overcome this supply problem. Going door to door with a borrowed camera in hand, he offered to make photographic portraits for a small fee, half now and half upon delivery of the photographs.

Using all his showmanship, the young man treated the customers more as an audience than as clients. The children laughed and giggled while the parents felt pride as he created the family's first photographs. After a long series of shots, the session was complete. The entrepreneur collected a small deposit, per the agreement.

He left the customer's home with money in his pocket and dashed off to the dry goods store to purchase film. The following day he arrived back at the customer's home, only this time with film in his camera. Apologetically explaining to them that the photographs would not develop, he offered to remake the entire session for no charge. Delighted that a door-to-door salesman would guarantee his product, the family happily reassembled and sat for another performance by the photographer.

At the appointed time, the photographer returned again to the customer's home. This time he had with him the precious photographs of the children and more of the family. Aided by the young salesman, the eager family made their selection of favorites and ordered more copies to give to loved ones.

Many years passed before the man turned his fledging venture into a profitable business, but at its peak, the company that bears his name, Olan Mills, Incorporated, laid claim to being *The Nation's Studio.*

Olan Mills's inventive approach to selling these portraits provided the stories that helped create the corporate culture that would eventually create an extraordinarily successful enterprise. But Olan was more than a sharp-dressing, smooth-talking salesman. He was, in addition, the pioneer that gave life and character to the portrait photography industry.

OLAN AND ME

I did not realize as a child how much I loved my grandfather nor how much his personality and the firm he founded and grew would mark my life. According to those individuals who called themselves his friends, he was a very likeable yet at times difficult man. Members of his own family, including his children, punctuate this fact. I knew him only as a grandfather.

I knew him in the storybook image of a grandfather. He would, without notice, pick me up from elementary school and take me away for weekends of fishing and boating. He carried me along on his business trips. When I was nine, he taught me to drive a stick shift Willy's jeep. Beginning at the age of 11, whenever I would accompany him on one of his private planes, I was his copilot. Together we built and painted, complete with a racing stripe, a special seat that raised me high enough to see over the dashboard of the cockpit. He also gave me my first job, with a weekly paycheck—Assistant to the Handyman.

We enjoyed each other's company, but most all, he spent time with me when I was an impressionable child. My grandfather was proud of me, and I basked in his attention. I still hold dear the memories of him acting as a surrogate father when my own father was away on business.

His children, unfortunately, did not all share these same warm memories. Instead, they suffered from his long absences, his womanizing ways, and his flawed personal relationships. Many of his faults may have been a result of his battle with alcohol, but many firms, as we will see, experience similar difficulties due to the personal idiosyncrasies and failings of a charismatic and powerful leader.

In 1972, following a stroke, my grandfather became unable to care for himself and moved in with his oldest daughter—my mother—and the rest of my immediate family. He and I lived in adjacent rooms upstairs in our North Dallas home. He, who had always taken care of me, suddenly needed me to care for many of his needs. It was a role reversal that served only to make us closer until April 15, 1978, the day he died. Although the effects on the business were far from my mind at the time, the experience has since provided a searing reminder of one inescapable fact of business leaders: eventually they all grow old and retire or die.

In the 25 years since my grandfather's death, I have spent a lot of time thinking about what he taught me—or better, what I learned from him. He never sat me down and extolled his views on technical issues like managing the balance sheets or increasing cash flow. Instead, he demonstrated how to build a child's self-esteem by allowing me to take risks and stand on my own feet. He was always building my confidence, boasting that I "could handle any piece of machinery (truck, tractor, airplane, boat, mower) at the lake ranch" or convincing me, an awkward teenager, how great I looked in my new plaid suit with red shirt, striped white tie, and white shoes to match.

He modeled for me the value of hard work. I look back at the very hot summer days spent working sunup to sundown and wonder how I might have turned out if I'd had it easy. One Saturday morning, he assigned me to dig a pit for the new cattle guard. He showed me where to dig and then jumped in his plane and flew back to Dallas for business. He returned around dusk, in time to inspect my day's work before nightfall. After seven hours of digging I had managed to dig a rectangular pit four feet wide by eight feet long and about seven feet deep. Rather than humiliate me (cattle guard pits need only be four or five inches deep), he was proud of me, citing my hard work and determination to get the job done. He didn't laugh at me for not knowing the correct depth. He instead picked up one of my shovels and began filling in my trench, exclaiming in the dark about what an excellent pit I had dug.

He taught me fairness. Although outwardly he gave the impression of living a charmed and exotic life, I believe his soul never left his poor farm upbringing. He had compassion for others less fortunate. He implemented a "Hire the Handicapped" policy in the early 60s, long before any governmental agency mandated such action. Although discrimination was common, he never showed this to me. One of his pilots, and one of my beloved mentors, eventually became totally deaf in both ears (back then pilots could easily circumvent communicating with control towers), telemarketing offices provided excellent jobs for the wheelchair bound, and women made up the vast majority of his total workforce.

One memorable employee that I worked shoulder to shoulder with for several years was a man by the name of Gabe. Gabe had been a professional boxer until he was drafted to serve in Vietnam. Gabe took a bullet in the head, and it lodged in such a way that the doctors decided to leave it undisturbed. Gabe lost most of his fine motor movement and some memory, and his speech became almost indecipherable. By the time he came to work for Olan Mills, Gabe was beaten down by these circumstances as well as from battling a lifetime of prejudice against African-Americans. Yet, years later, in part because of my grandfather's acceptance of him as a person, he was able to live a dignified and in many ways successful life.

One of the most vivid lessons my grandfather demonstrated was the benefit of strong determination and a positive attitude. He ingrained in me an outlook of, "Anything you do in life, you can do better with a positive attitude." He showed me the power of believing in myself. This belief, while common among most entrepreneurs, is rare among the general population. Although he never taught me to swing a golf club or throw a fastball, he showed me the same determination that world class athletes live by in their quest to be the best. He started a business with only his wits and grew it to become a household name, along the way meeting and beating back hundreds, if not thousands, of obstacles. Olan Mills, Inc., nearly went broke several times before it finally found its legs. Discipline and determination are the foundations of any successful individual, whether in business, sports, or personal relationships. I have witnessed this lesson hundreds of times when employees mouth the words of success but then give up in the face of obstacles. Most want simply to be placed at the top and not overcome the numerous obstacles that are inherent in the journey.

Unknown to him, he also taught me through his shortcomings. For a man that was living the real American Dream, Granddad was unhappy in his later years. I look back over our time together and realize that he lived an unbalanced life. Life was work, and when work was down, so was he. The Christmas season is loaded with profit for most retail concerns, and Olan Mills, Inc., was no different. For many, this time of year turns nine months of loss into a profit. Yet, like clockwork, he would go into a depressed mood at the end of the Christmas retail season. I couldn't count on him to celebrate birthdays and holidays. I never witnessed him praying, attending church, or sporting events. He worked.

Granddad didn't teach me business lessons: he taught me life lessons. He was and still is one of my greatest mentors. His lessons influenced several concepts in this book—the role of self-esteem in leadership, giving later generations room to grow, having passion for what you do, and keeping clear chains of command. He opened my young eyes to the inevitable complications of business life.

OLAN MILLS, INC., AND ME

My career at Olan Mills, Inc., began at the very bottom of the ladder, as a part-time, split-shift telemarketer. We called the work *smilin' and dialin'* or *rollin' with Olan,* and while few found it pleasant, I turned out to have a marked gift for selling photography over the phone. I went on to work at Olan Mills, Inc., in virtually every capacity—photographer, sales consultant, even janitor. My heart was not set on a career with Olan Mills, Inc., but between college graduation and graduate school, I was solicited to work in the business as a corporate trainee, a position where I could not only learn every phase of operations but also assume responsibility for troubled units. My first project was a small group of grossly under-performing stores in the Boston area, an assignment riddled with problems—a genuine turnaround. Accepting help from a number of new hires, we began showing modest profits for the first time—mission accomplished. With the Boston success behind me, I began rising through the ranks as a sales supervisor, area manager, district manager, and regional manager. Eventually, I held full responsibility for leading and managing all of Olan Mills Studios, the company's largest operating unit.

I spent nearly 20 years working in a highly successful business, and I know firsthand how attitudes among owners, leaders, and others involved in business can develop and change for good or ill. The building of any great business or financial empire has its trade-offs. For example, when a family is involved, the trade-off is usually business growth at the expense of the family. As the business grows, family relations become more complex and remote. As a family business grows, the prospect of maintaining "normal" family relations becomes even dimmer. Unfortunately, my professional experience as a business consultant bears witness to this reality.

During my years with Olan Mills, Inc., we gave to each other. The company gave me travel, excitement, and, within a small circle, recognition. I achieved a comfortable lifestyle. Most of all, the company gave me opportunity, while I gave it virtually all my time and energy, frequently putting my wife and children second to the demands of building and steering an increasingly successful business. My emotional loyalty rested as much with the company as it did with my family. We were consumed with each other. I was a faithful employee and steward of the business. It was a long and happy affair.

Then one morning I woke up in deep pain, and realized that Olan Mills, Inc., and I had changed. The honeymoon was over. Time had passed and we were no longer suited for each other. The necessities of my life had been satisfied, but I was still, as the psychologist Abraham Maslow might say, searching for self-actualization. Continuing that search would mean going in a completely new direction, and I knew if I were to start over again, my wife and children might have to give up a level of security as well as some comforts.

Leaving a business where you have prospered for many years is difficult, if not outright impossible. Why did I do it? A primary reason was that the personal and family business issues at Olan Mills,

Inc., had become crushingly intense. Lacking clarity, mired in outdated techniques, and confused by poor communication, I was unsure where to go next. I reasoned that the only thing worse than working in the same business for 20 years and knowing I would leave, was to be there for 25 years and leave. I decided to leave.

I gave back my executive and operational responsibilities and general manager duties in January 1995. Although it was certainly no joke, I formally resigned on April 1, 1995. I signed the necessary papers and returned the package on April 15th, the 17th anniversary of my grandfather's death. The following morning, I woke up as usual and did something I had often thought about but had seldom done in 19 years; I rolled over and went back to sleep.

To leave a long-time employer can be like awakening from a trance. It sometimes seemed to me as if the experience of working at Olan Mills had happened to someone else. As a business consultant, I see these dynamics at work in other firms. Because the emotional lives of the leaders are so tightly integrated with the business, they easily become blinded to reality.

For all its inherent difficulties, however, to spend your working life laboring happily alongside people you know, respect, and love is the finest experience in the world. I remember fondly many of my years with Olan Mills, Inc., and can only wish that others might experience a similar level of personal joy and professional satisfaction. I can say with absolute certainty that investing the time and energy to achieve professional satisfaction is worthwhile, and only through this investment will sustainable business success ever become a reality.

REGENERATION

I realized early in life that change was inevitable. I never visualized that I would devote my entire professional career to Olan Mills, Inc., Frankly, this prospect seemed unattractive. My dream was to have several careers. Through constantly starting anew and beginning fresh, I hoped always to have an unbinding passion, interest, and enthusiasm for work. I was, after all, trying to regenerate[1] personally. After the experience of working in a closely held enterprise while contributing and leading explosive growth through 19 years, I realized that I had much to share with other leaders of closely held enterprises. I dedicated myself, with the same passion that I learned from Granddad and practiced at Olan Mills, to helping other business leaders generate the same type of energy, actions, and thinking required for long-term success.

Following my passion, I set up shop in 1995. I struggled with a company name, because I did not want people retaining my new firm and expecting me to solve their problems based solely on my narrow industry success or, worse yet, a recognizable name. In fact, I have rejected all photographic-related industry consulting opportunities. Instead, I wanted to work with closely held enterprises and their leaders in a partnership, whereby I could assist them in their learning how to achieve sustainable success. In other words, I wanted to help them regenerate. After six months, the name of my new enterprise suddenly became obvious: ReGENERATION Partners.

Today, I have gone deep into the process of organizing and systematizing the knowledge and experience that I have gained from working in my own family business, from serving as an interim CEO of several companies (including a dotcom), and from my consultation with leaders of other companies. Without a doubt, my greatest source of education has been my clients.

During my years with Olan Mills, Inc., I received tremendous joy from rolling up my sleeves and leading the charge for achieving team success. Now, I receive the same joy from advising and

---

[1]*American Heritage Dictionary:* to reform spiritually or morally; to form, create, construct anew; restored; refreshed.

coaching other leaders on how they can better construct and lead their own teams to achieve long-term, sustainable success. By focusing my energies on sharing my business experiences with others, I am realizing a dream. My work with various clients is constantly changing and starting fresh. I am constantly experiencing the joy of regeneration.

In this process, I am fortunate to have associates of ReGENERATION Partners that constantly keep me on my toes and add greatly to the intellectual capital of the firm. These individuals are among the very best and brightest I have encountered in any firm. I am blessed beyond words.

In my personal life, I look at my two sons from a new perspective and wonder what lessons they are learning. My elder son's middle name, like mine, is Olan; my younger son's middle name is Mills. They tell friends their middle names together are *Olan Mills*. Already, I've placed a mark upon them of the business that marked me.

Many people author books about their own accomplishments. A great many more books are written about famous and illustrative figures from the objective perspective of an outsider. *Portraits of Success* is different. Somewhat like a professional photographer taking pictures of his own family, it combines an insider's intimate firsthand knowledge and experience with an outsider's objective perspective.

The issues surrounding every closely held business mark the future of the owners, employees, stakeholders, and communities, just as the gilt Olan Mills signature marks snapshots in millions of pocketbooks and wallets. This book is written to show that those issues can be dealt with and that, like those gold-embossed photos, a business enterprise can be a source of prosperity, security, and memories to last a lifetime—and beyond.

Building Companies That Last

A search of any electronic database of books will reveal scores of titles containing the words *business* or *success*. Everybody, it often seems, is looking for the keys to business success—and almost as many are offering it. *Portraits of Success* doesn't propose a single key, however, nor is the plan presented for everybody.

Portraits of Success offers an approach for business leaders with profit-and-loss responsibility. I interpret that broadly to include owners, CEOs, CFOs, and senior executives as well as department heads. It's for leaders who have a long-term perspective, those who look beyond the next quarterly numbers or other short-range financial goals.

It's also for leaders who are managing and leading going concerns with the necessary financial controls already in place. My plan is not to advise companies in critical turnaround situations or startups where the aim is to cash out quickly through an initial public offering or sale of the company. *Portraits of Success* is intended to enable healthy businesses survive long term, through leadership cultivation and succession. These words will have the greatest impact on leaders building companies, not looking for immediate monetization—and for making them last decades, not helping them survive the next few weeks.

Portraits of Success is designed and appropriate for an exceptionally broad audience of leaders, companies, and industries. In my long career, I have worked with, and so direct my comments toward, closely held firms, including family-owned enterprises. Managers and leaders of small and medium-sized companies as well as those in multibillion-dollar corporations can practice and profit from these concepts—and have. These concepts have been honed in companies that manufacture, distribute, or provide a service within industries as diverse as agriculture and ranching to telecommunications, from health care to food service, all with positive results. Furthermore, the advisors to all these firms, including bankers, accountants, attorneys, consultants, private equity fund managers, and financial planners are ideal audiences for *Portraits of Success.*

The power of the concepts lies in their comprehensiveness coupled with a refreshing simplicity. My clients have taught me that advice does not have to be complicated to be good. For example, washing your hands is regarded by many medical experts to be the single greatest advancement in the history of health care. Simple, yet profound. Occam's Razor is a theory that states that, given essentially equal choices, the simplest choice is the best. So it often is with successful business decisions.

These concepts, however, don't cover every issue faced by a company. You won't find anything here about spurring innovative product development or managing rapid international expansion, for instance. The common thread in these concepts is humanity. They are about people—managing and leading people, helping people achieve, allowing them to be happy, and encouraging them to work together productively. I have seen and I believe, given a sound business concept along with adequate capitalization and financial controls, that people are the greatest advantage in the long-term survival and success of every business.

WHAT IS SUCCESS?

As a nation, we obsess about achieving success. We talk about it and read about it. We watch and listen to others who claim to "have it" more than any other people on Earth. How to get it, how to keep it, how to enjoy it, and even, for some, how to keep our enemies from it have become the preoccupation and pastime for millions of Americans. The techniques and stories of success dominate the news and reportage of business, entertainment, politics, sports, and even personal relationships. It has always been so, and we are always going to talk about success in this way. But lost in the ongoing debate is the answer to a key question: *What is success?*

Some view success in the same manner as pornography, saying, "I'll know it when I see it." The problem with this flexible attitude is that the criteria are too fuzzy and shift with each new development. Because many don't have a clear map to success, they will almost certainly drift off course during the journey. Like the captain of the sailboat with no destination in mind, any wind is the right wind. For these people, *Portraits of Success* will have immediate and obvious application.

No matter how you view success, the first important step is to write your own definition. Success is not a one-size-fits-all proposition. For instance, one person's success may consist of getting and keeping a lifelong job. For another, success may be realized by working at a wide variety of interesting positions. Others find success in their private life, considering a good marriage and well-adjusted children to be the only real standard. Others want it all.

In addition to the obvious personal differences in the way success is defined, there are very likely to be generational differences. That is, members of one generation will tend to define success one

way, while another sees it quite differently. One such gap exists between members of the Depression era generation and the Boomers.
Depression-born adults tend to define success in terms of security,
while the Boomer generation often considers consumption the primary criteria.

Regardless, we can all agree that we are after success. When you
are talking about a closely held business, you are talking about a
group effort. Even in a sole proprietorship dominated by a charismatic owner-founder, at least several people are needed to drive
the company forward, and in nearly every case, there will eventually be a larger number of owners. So having consensus about success is important, because that is, after all, the goal.

First, let's define what success is *not*. In a closely held enterprise,
success is of necessity more than wealth, more than creating a global enterprise, more than recognition. Next, let's be inclusive,
drawing a line around the major stakeholders in our success definition. This is straightforward: individual, family, and business
success are inextricably linked. The question of whether you are
personally enjoying the rewards of a full meaningful life is just as
critical as the company's balance sheet. In fact, from a personal
perspective, your happiness is likely far more important than any
corporate success.

DEFINING INDIVIDUAL SUCCESS

Individual success is the continued realization of worthwhile
accomplishments or goals. It means that you feel good about what
you do and that you are continuing to grow spiritually, emotionally, physically, or financially. Within that broad definition of individual success, several different varieties exist, ranging from the
person who doesn't seem to have any goals at all, to the one who
works toward specific goals without apparently ever achieving
them.

Sometimes, an individual may define his success by the successes of others. Teachers often fall into this group, measuring their own achievements as educators by the academic accomplishments of their pupils. Coaches, trainers, family business owners, and managers are also likely to measure their success by the successes of their athletes, trainees, offspring, and employees.

Continuously realizing worthwhile goals may sound like a pretty tough target. Indeed, many people go long periods without achieving any of the highly placed goals they have set for themselves. A teenage science student who sets her heart on becoming an astronaut, a mother who wants to watch her daughter marry a doctor, or a business school graduate who covets a corner office may, unfortunately, never see these dreams realized. But these people may still experience significant success by progressing at least part of the way toward the goals they have chosen. This demonstrates an often overlooked aspect of success, namely that it isn't an all-or-nothing proposition. A measure of success, or even progress towards a goal, can be very satisfying.

People calculating their individual success may measure themselves against goals that no one else sees, or that are so fuzzily or idiosyncratically defined that, for other people, they simply don't exist. For instance, a parent or grandparent may define success as being a good parent or grandparent, and they very likely have no specific measurements by which to calculate how well they're succeeding. They do not, in other words, count the hugs and verbal gratitude they receive from their offspring and plot a graph to see how well they are doing.

But these people are still achieving individual success, on their own terms, by having worthwhile goals and continuously achieving them, or at least making progress toward achieving them. On the most important scale of all, they know success when they experience it.

Having Fun at Work

Are you happy? Do you experience the normal ebb and flow of life? It is very difficult for anybody to continue working effectively and successfully unless he is personally happy. Of course, we all know people who grimly persist, forcing themselves to go to work or even to get out of bed in the morning in the face of seemingly intractable dissatisfaction. But this mode of living is not sustainable—not in the long run. More importantly, no one who is genuinely successful is chronically unhappy.

Even a professional acrobat has difficulty making progress while hopping on one foot. How much more difficult is it to make progress in business and life when all the emphasis is placed on what "must be done" and never on what generates fun. Finding a sense of fun at your work is critical, as it is a basic component in long-term business success.

Having a Balanced Life

There is more to life than work, and there is also more to life than play. The life of the successful business leader should be multifaceted. Business leaders have opportunities and, indeed, responsibilities to participate and contribute to their communities, charities, churches, education, hobbies and avocations, and, of course, their families. The musician Bruce Springsteen addressed this when, after his divorce, he said, "I have learned that giving 100 percent to my music is not giving 100 percent of my life to my music."

When you prepare a list of goals for the coming week, year, and life, think about balance. If you consider only financial objectives, you are likely to achieve only financial goals. If you provide a balanced set of objectives, the odds of your achieving a balanced success—the kind of success that keeps individuals, families, and businesses percolating for decades—will be greatly enhanced.

Making a Contribution

Self-esteem, about which more will be said, is the consequence of making a worthwhile contribution. Let's set aside for a moment the issue of your contribution to your family, your business, and your society. Human experience varies so widely, even among the relatively narrow group of closely held business leaders, that it's hard and, frankly, not productive for me to tell you how you should contribute. The choice is very personal.

You are an expert, the only expert, on what you want. So define your contribution in a way that is most appropriate to you. It may be employing as many family members as possible, or providing quality goods and services at fair prices to the world market, or simply generating wealth, which you charitably donate where you think best. However you decide to contribute, pick something personally worthwhile, and then do it.

Building Wealth

A business should be a security creator and wealth creator, not a destroyer. Of course, many businesses turn out to be only the latter. The founder or perhaps a risk-loving investor, starts with seed money and in a short time has run through the start-up capital without generating sufficient profits to keep the business going.

Many family businesses are nearly the exact opposite, however. They generate a steady growth in the family wealth, generation after generation, increasing the overall level of the family's prosperity even when, as is usual, the number of owners and employees increase with each generation. This kind of wealth building is what you should envision for your closely held business. Consistent, long-lasting growth in wealth is perhaps the first and foremost component of business success.

DEFINING BUSINESS SUCCESS

Business success, like family success, is very hard to nail down. For some businesses, success may be staying afloat in a highly competitive field; for others, it may be nothing less than dominating the global market for their product. However, these are mainly differences of degree.

Profits have to flow in without serious or continued disruption over a significant time if the business is to remain viable. This is a basic law of business, one that is not changed when the business assets are large or when past income has been substantial. All businesses must be managed profitably if they are to succeed.

That said, when it comes to profitability, flexibility is one of the hallmarks of closely held enterprises. Generally, these businesses are not subject to the short-term orientation of firms financed in the public capital markets. They need not manipulate their operations and plans to show quarter by quarter profit increases to please Wall Street analysts.

That flexibility, incidentally, provides a significant competitive edge. Family-owned Mars, for instance, required net profit margins of only 3 percent on any new products or investments. No public company could possibly consider such anemic returns. Yet Mars has grown to be the world's largest candy company as well as one of the most profitable by taking this conservative approach to steady, if not explosive, profitability.

Achieving Consistent Growth

Many, many companies have literally grown themselves to death. Cash flow does not equal profits. When the payables cycle is shorter that the receivables cycle, when inventory must be bought now for sale later, when materials have to be ordered today for sales that won't be booked for a year—under these common if not universal circumstances, out-of-control growth can lead to cash crunches, bankruptcy, and disaster. Closely held firms, lacking easy access to public equity capital markets, are in even worse shape than other firms when it comes to dealing with too-rapid growth.

The only answer is not, despite what you read in the financial journals, to go public or sell the company to investors and continue the race for breakneck growth. Another solution, which many firms have found viable for long-term success, is to constrain growth, to keep it moderate, consistent, and manageable. Companies which find themselves in steadily growing markets, or that show a knack for consistently finding new, appropriately growing market niches, will avoid the specter of uncontrolled growth that has sunk many firms. Achieving consistent growth is a major factor in long-term success in closely held firms.

Slaying Success

The concept of failure, the theoretical opposite of success, can be difficult to understand. We can usually define the moment, the decision, or the act that enabled success, such as the winning putt on the 18th hole, or the decision to put it all on the Las Vegas tables á la Fred Smith of FedEx. But failure is more difficult to pinpoint. Business failure is caused by numerous events, decisions, or circumstances, but overall, the most common reasons fall into one or more of the following categories.

Concept. Many companies are based on a poor business concept where the value proposition isn't financially sound. The idea may pitch well—it may sound exciting and innovative—but the reality is often as simply put as the answer to the question: Do we really need a better mousetrap? The answer, of course, is *no* or, at best, *not particularly.* Discerning real consumer purchasing practices from wishful thinking is more difficult than it sounds.

Planning. The journey of a thousand miles certainly does start with a single step, but on the whole, that first step is going to be the easiest of the trip. In other words, planning the long-term success of a bright idea is usually more difficult than coming up with the bright idea in the first place. Such long-term business planning is far more complex than a simple business plan. It will include plans for managing growth, risk, and wealth, and the means to ensure succession as well as a well-conceived, lasting estate. None of these issues are easy, but neither are they insurmountable.

Inexperienced management. A wooden stake for many a promising company is inexperienced management. How many dotcoms failed because the 21-year-old CEO with a great idea and a wonderful computer staff had no idea how to manage the company to the next level? We'll never know, but you can be certain there were more than a few. In any new promising company, a time comes when you must transition from the founding team, often entrepreneurs, to one with professionals who are more experienced in making the business a long-term success.

Capital. Or lack thereof. The saying goes that it takes money to make money, and it's never been truer. Every company must have the resources to survive a downturn in its market or pay for an essential expansion. More companies probably fail for lack of capital than for any other reason.

Although it may appear obvious that a lack of capital will drive a company into bankruptcy, I am not referring to running out of cash, like overdrawing a checking account. Consider the upstart Legend Airways competing against the mighty American Airlines.

OUT OF FOCUS
_____

Legend Airlines

Legend Airlines may not be the best name for the upstart
aviation company that began flying out of Dallas's Love Field
Airport, less than ten minutes from my home. Legend flew for
less than a year before declaring bankruptcy in December 2000.
Only a few months later, it was forced to surrender its license to
operate and thus disappeared once and for all over the horizon.
It never grew very big, operating only a handful of commercial
jets offering luxury service between Dallas and New York, Los
Angeles, and Washington, D.C., at Comfort Inn prices. While
many young technology companies were able to raise unseemly
amounts of capital on the strength of nebulous Internet concepts,
this airline's seasoned managers were unable to generate
enough investor backing to keep it aloft more than eight months.

Yet Legend does have a tale worth telling. It's a tale about
money, pure and simple. Legend had almost everything going
for it: a brave idea, solid leadership, a large and eager market,
and a proven business concept. It possessed admirable moxie,
demonstrated by the years-long legal battle required to
overcome a federal law that prohibited long-distance flights out
of Love Field. Legend's brave idea was to reconfigure airliners to
contain no more than 56 seats—the limit set by the Wright
Amendment passed to protect Dallas/Fort Worth Airport from
competition at Love Field many years earlier—and make them
all first-class supple leather, foot rest included.

It did that with style. The modified aircraft sported individual
satellite TVs with each seat, great food served on real china, a
good choice of wines, no carry-on limit, and top-shelf service. I
was a particular fan of the airline, because it allowed me to reach

clients on either coast via a private secured parking garage and nonstop flights minutes from my front door.

Unfortunately for Legend, their fans didn't include American Airlines. The Wright Amendment was passed to protect Dallas/ Fort Worth Airport from competition, meaning, in essence, to protect American, far and away the dominant carrier there. American kept Legend tied up in court for as long as it could, taking its efforts all the way to the Supreme Court.

Legend ultimately beat American in court, but it couldn't overcome the shadow of the looming aviation giant on Wall Street. Legend was never adequately capitalized as a start-up. Because the possible threat of legal defeat was never completely dispelled, the company was unable to attract continuing capital. Legend ultimately wound up owing $18.7 million in unsecured debt, and when a last-ditch effort to raise $20 million to keep it going failed, met its end.

Legend may have failed as an airline, but it succeeds as a fable. This fable illustrates that money matters. No matter how good the idea, how smart the management, or how promising the market, if you don't possess the capital to keep a business running long enough to become self-sustaining, you won't make it. I think about this story frequently as I'm driving the 45 minutes to the terminal at Dallas/Fort Worth airport, and then later on a plane, squeezing into a middle seat, balancing my laptop on my knees. It's a good lesson to recall.

THE NINE KEYS TO SUSTAINABLE SUCCESS

To achieve success, one must gain a solid understanding of the role of self-esteem in business leadership. Once we've grasped this Key, we can move on to the other eight Keys. Here is a first look at the nine Keys. Each will be explored in depth in a separate chapter.

Key 1: The Secret of Great Business Leadership

It's no secret that scions of successful entrepreneurs often make lousy executives, or that few people can lead a company as well as its founder. But why is that? The reason could be described as *The Secret of Great Business Leadership.* The unpleasant reality is that later-generation failure is often rooted in the way the founder and his employees treat those who will one day lead the company. It makes no difference whether they are members of the majority-owning family or promising leaders selected and groomed for success. The single biggest failure of businesses when it comes to grooming successors is the corrosive effect the founder and/or his subordinates have on the personal self-esteem of the anointed future leaders. Being on the fast track, it turns out, can be a strong negative indicator for future competence.

That's why the first Key, and in many ways the most important one, is the directive to nurture high self-esteem in future leaders. Building self-esteem is largely a matter of doing what *doesn't* come naturally when it comes to nurturing future leaders. Instead of coddling them with cushy assignments and protecting them with low-risk jobs, you build self-esteem by giving them challenges and requiring that they take risks. In the course of building self-esteem, you will inevitably uncover weaknesses in your chosen future leaders. In some cases, these road-tested executives may fail, and that's unfortunate. But the only way to improve the dismal long-term survival statistics for companies, it turns out, is to increase the challenging, testing, and boosting of self-esteem in those who would lead.

Key 2: Make It a Meritocracy

When I landed my first job in the business where I would spend the first part of my professional life, the thought that crossed my mind was not, "I deserve this." but, "Thanks, Mom." Given that

I showed up late, out of breath, dirty and soaked with perspiration after my 12-year-old car died in a busy intersection during the rush hour heat of a Phoenix summer, I might well have been turned away from my first day of work—but for the fact that my mother was Olan Mills's daughter.

As it turned out, I rose to the top ranks of Olan Mills's executives—at least in part through merit, I like to think. But you can't count on such benign outcomes from the popular practice of automatically hiring and instantly promoting employees merely or mainly because they belong to the right family, went to the right college, belong to the right ethnic group, or otherwise conform to some characteristic not related to merit.

Unfortunately, making a business a true meritocracy isn't as simple as putting a halt to the automatic hiring and promotion of the founder's grandchildren. Meritocracy is sabotaged by all kinds of things other than genetic relationships. Companies that hire and promote executives based entirely, or partly, on their gender, religion, ethnic background, age, or educational background are doing the same thing and will suffer for it. To create a meritocracy, you have to be sensitive to preferential treatment in all its forms, and stamp it out for the long-range good of the enterprise.

Key 3: Give the Next Generation Room to Grow

While I was a competent executive at Olan Mills, Inc., I have benefited enormously from in-depth consulting relationships with numerous other businesses and the multiple interim CEO roles I have filled for various enterprises since I left Olan Mills. This experience highlights the errors that many businesses make in limiting their employees's growth. They may prevent employees from working elsewhere, fail to recruit former employees back to the company, or neglect opportunities to have employees work closely with customers and suppliers.

Whatever the specific ingredients, this recipe will dumb down the business's intellectual capital. You lead best when you hire and develop people with character and integrity and give them room to grow. Letting them see other ways of doing things allows them to experience the consequences of their own decisions. These and other simple techniques will increase the intelligence of the organization to its long-term benefit.

This may sound impractical, but businesses can take specific actions to give future generations room to grow. These include engaging in joint ventures with other firms, sharing employees with customers and suppliers, and even allowing ex-employees to get job experience elsewhere, then return to the company.

Key 4: Find a Common Direction

Two watershed events in Olan Mills's history occurred when homemakers began entering the workforce in large numbers and, as a result, the use of answering machines began to grow exponentially across America. This combination meant big trouble for Olan Mills's longstanding reliance on telemarketing to attract customers. The company probably could have negotiated this obstacle more effectively had management agreed to a single corrective course. Some feared the collapse of telemarketing via legislation and wanted out of phoning altogether. Others believed the company needed to plow more resources into telemarketing.

The result was an impasse and no significant change, which resulted in a loss of market share. This setback was predictable, because business success is unlikely without leadership communicating both a shared vision and common goals on everything from marketing methods to the business's basic purpose. The idea is not to snuff out discussion, but only when those in charge agree on the basics does a company prosper.

Finding a common direction isn't always easy. It can mean some hard choices, sometimes involving the departure of leaders who can't join the common endeavor. Other times, you may be able to get everyone on the same page simply by identifying and highlighting the precise differences between viewpoints, then getting those involved to agree to disagree for the sake of the enterprise. It isn't necessarily easy, but it is vital.

Key 5: Make Communication Central

Dysfunctional relationships and incompatible communication styles exist in all companies and can only be overcome by making effective communication a central concern. My experience in dealing with especially troublesome communication issues has led me to understand how important communication is and how it can be improved even in the most challenging circumstances.

To a considerable degree, making communication central is less a collection of specific techniques than a broad mindset that must shape everything that the company does. Sure, starting a company newsletter may help communication, or at least appear to, but if leaders continue to protect their fiefdoms, hide information from others, and carry hidden agendas, then cosmetic communication remedies will fail to build a company that endures.

Key 6: Cultivate Passion and Balance

Olan Mills was every inch the driven, imaginative, forceful, and passionate image of the stereotypical entrepreneur. Under his leadership, as is usual with founders, passion was never an issue. As time passed and the reins were handed down to others, however, it became clear that keeping that level of passion alive among a larger group would present a greater challenge.

The loss of innovative energy is a problem common to all businesses as they grow and mature. Yet no business whose leaders are mere caretakers is positioned for long-term success or, frankly, even survival. Clearly, some way must be found to create and maintain the passionate interest and involvement of later generations.

Perhaps the simplest way is simply to show your own passion. Business leaders don't have to be buttoned-down and unemotional—not when the long-term survival of their company is at stake. One of the most successful companies in history is Microsoft, which almost since its inception has boasted the leadership of Steve Ballmer. Now CEO of the software juggernaut, Ballmer is legendary for his outsized expressions of passion about Microsoft, its products, its people, and its prospects. When you communicate with people in your company, be certain that some expression of your passion is included regularly in your remarks.

Key 7: Create Business Traditions, Myths and Shared Beliefs

When Olan Mills, Inc., first tried to expand from its home base in Tuscaloosa, Alabama, into nearby Greenville, Alabama, the company nearly collapsed. Although less than 200 miles away, the initial Greenville campaign was such a disaster that the sales team, although headed by the talented founder, recorded zero sales in the first week. The disheartened employees, demanding to return home to Tuscaloosa, were then shocked to learn that Olan Mills had placed their personal belongings as guarantee against the rooming house charges! With difficulty, the charismatic Mills convinced the discouraged salespeople to try again—and then, to make his point, signed that same rooming house's proprietor as the first portrait customer.

From this shaky initial attempt at expansion, company lore has it, Olan Mills, Inc., became the world's largest portrait photography company with operations throughout the United States, Canada, and Great Britain. It's a powerful story and illustrates the importance of risk taking and perseverance to all Olan Mills's employees in dramatic fashion.

Myths and traditions like this are key to business culture and to building the shared beliefs that enable employees to deal with complex, changing business issues in a consistent manner. Myths may seem to spring from nowhere and have lives of their own, but the truth is they can be encouraged and molded to meet the needs of a business. If it lacks a folksy means to tell and retell the company culture, whether stressing the importance of self-discipline, the value of people, or the worth of hard work, a business is in for tough times over the long haul.

Key 8: Do the Strongest Really Survive?

Consider for a moment a few of the companies that were once number one in their fields and now are no more. There is Pullman, once synonymous with railroad sleeper cars in the way Xerox today is with photocopying. Pan American was once the world's largest airline but today survives only in memory. Montgomery Ward, although it never surpassed its rival Sears, was in position to challenge Sears & Roebuck at the end of World War II, but was driven into bankruptcy in 1997 and disappeared.

These are legends, truly vast enterprises that loomed over entire industries and even whole economies. Yet they met their ends just as surely as much smaller enterprises and, in fact, were survived by many former competitors who were much smaller.

The purpose of this chapter is to examine what causes this phenomenon and to advance the theory that adaptability, more than size or strength, is the most important characteristic for companies that prevail and endure.

Key 9: Managing Risk

It's surprising, if you read business biographies, how many noted businesspeople were also noted card players. H.L. Hunt, Warren Buffett, and countless other entrepreneurs and business legends were nonpareils around a card table. Why? The common element in succeeding in business, as well as in practical probabilities inherent in such games as poker, is the ability to assess risk accurately and quickly.

This chapter looks at the importance of assessing risk and considers some of the tools for its appropriate management. It will help business leaders recognize, first, that risk always exists, even when they don't recognize it. Second, it helps them to find ways to manage risk in any business scenario by controlling the elements they can control and minimizing their exposure to uncontrollable risk.

USING THE KEYS

It is not necessary to implement all, or any, of the nine Keys at once. This system is not one that must be put into place wholesale or not at all. That's not modesty; it's simple reality. No single system can tell in detail how every company should be run; one size does not fit all. Businesses are too varied and too complex for any single plan to work across the board. Take what you need from the nine Keys now and reserve the rest for when, and if, you need them.

Regardless of when you implement any of the Keys, I believe you can get the most value from them by executing the following four steps:

1. *Read* Portraits of Success *once all the way through to absorb the overall message.* Some of the Keys deal with interrelated problems. Although you may become enthused about applying one of the Keys as soon as you read about it, wait until you

have studied the others before determining which Key is appropriate for your situation.

2. *Recognize where you need help.* This should be easy—the fact that you are reading this book means you are open to having problem areas pointed out and probably have a few in mind already. But again, as you study the Keys, you are very likely to become aware of improvements in areas you felt were already doing fine. Retain that openness and keep focused on the goal of creating long-term success rather than in protecting the status quo.

3. *Work on problem areas. Portraits of Success* does not purport to describe a painless regimen, and its subject matter is sweeping, more sweeping than you might initially realize. So even if you feel your firm would benefit from the application of all nine Keys, be cautious before attempting such a profound modification. Focus on the three or four areas where you think you will get the biggest long-term bang for your investment of time and energy. When you have those programs underway and see results from your efforts, move on to the next set.

4. *Reread and repeat. Portraits of Success* is more a philosophical treatise than a beach read, and every aspect of its message is not readily apparent. It's not intended to jazz you up for a few weeks and then dissipate, so you go back to your old ways of doing things and a limited, short-term future. Instead, it is intended to reward those who read and reread it, obtaining a greater insight into the requirements of long-term success with each exposure. So come back again, every month, every quarter, or every year to see what answers you can find for new problems that have cropped up and may threaten your company's prospects for a long-term, profitable existence.

CHAPTER 1

The Secret of Great Business Leadership

It was dinnertime in the home of a family whose patriarch had founded and built from scratch one of the largest independent oil producers in the state of Colorado. As the tall, powerful, charismatic entrepreneur settled into his place at the head of the table and reached for a serving spoon, the youngest of his three children at the table cleared his throat.

The founder, gray-haired but still as physically forceful as when he had played professional sports, halted, frowned, and rumbled impatiently, "What is it?"

The son, in his early 20s, had inherited his father's craggy looks and strong frame and was about to graduate from college, but his voice quavered as he told his father that he was considering going to work for another company after graduation. Instead of launching into an account of the excellent reasons he had for making the move, he let his words trail off and lapsed into an awkward silence, waiting for the storm.

But instead of exploding into a tirade, his father merely ladled a helping onto his plate and searched through some of the other bowls on the table. After a moment he turned to face his son, laughed and shook his head. "Now why would you want to do that?" he asked, scorn dripping thick as gravy. The son shrank back into his seat while his sisters shot him I-told-you-so glances. That was the last time the matter was brought up.

Instead of joining another company, the son submissively followed his two older sisters into the family business, occupying a corner office and exercising his expensive education with busy-work that any of a dozen staff members could have handled admirably. As time passed and no responsibility came his way, he again followed his older sisters' example by leaving the office early—to play golf or begin long weekends. He began taking extended vacations each season and gradually distanced himself from even the semblance of business responsibility.

The founder grumbled to himself occasionally when his son's indolence caught his attention. He would then dive back into his work, and everyone would forget the matter—until the day he died suddenly of a massive heart attack, leaving the company in the hands of his son.

What happened next probably shouldn't surprise anybody. The image of the wastrel scion of a successful entrepreneur taking over and quickly destroying what had been a healthy and fruitful enterprise is firmly ingrained in our business tradition. In fact, it seems we're surprised when a second or later generation business executive doesn't turn out to be incompetent. "Why can't Johnny work like his dad?" is a nearly constant refrain in the business world.

But the pace and scope of the destruction wrought by the son's bad judgement and sheer incompetence in the wake of his father's death was, in this case, exceptionally speedy and complete. Within a few years, the son sold what was left of the once thriving family business for 5 percent of what had been its value when the old man was alive. Most of those who watched the debacle just chalked it up to the curse of the second generation and left it at that.

Of course, there is no such curse. Many enterprises are managed successfully over long periods of time by leaders handpicked, if not genetically sired, by company founders. This includes companies as diverse as the Walt Disney Co., ably steered by Roy Disney after the death of his uncle Walt, and Playboy Enterprises, where Hugh Hefner's daughter Christie holds the CEO's title. Many well known car dealers, plumbing companies, homebuilders, and other enterprises in your own community and throughout the world all thrive in the caring and capable hands of next-generation leaders. Indeed, it can be argued that the exception makes the rule.

There are, of course, many reasons why one business thrives while another withers. Many of these reasons are only one step removed or just slightly beyond the control of the companies's leaders. Economic trends, changing consumer tastes, the collapse or emergence of competitors, acts of God, and even terrorism can all strike and leave even the best-managed companies and industries in chaos.

However, a once thriving business collapses in the hands of later generation leadership more often because control has been left in the hands of people who have never been allowed to do the job. As a result, on some very personal level, they don't believe they can do the job, so they don't.

That's where self-esteem enters the picture.

It's hard to blame business people if they don't understand the value of self-esteem. Many outside the business world don't understand its value either. People's attitudes toward self-respect, self-worth, self-esteem, and a sense of the *self* in general vary, and vary a lot. Even the experts who study the role of self-esteem in our lives arrive at very different conclusions.

The concept of self-esteem isn't new. The philosopher George Santayana pounded self-esteem into the dirt when he wrote, "Perhaps the only true dignity of man is his capacity to despise himself." Essayist Joan Didion hit a high one to the opposite field stating, "To have that sense of one's intrinsic worth, which constitutes self-respect, is potentially to have everything: the ability to discriminate, to love, and to remain indifferent. To lack it is to be locked within oneself, paradoxically incapable of either love or indifference." Mark Twain once said, "When people do not respect us, we are sharply offended; yet deep down in his private heart, no man much respects himself."

Regardless of the judgement concerning self-esteem, the weight of professional opinion says that it is very important to us. David Burns, a psychiatrist, depression researcher, and author of self-help books, places low self-esteem at the heart of a wide range of psychological problems, from suicidal impulses to troubled marriages. "Self-esteem is one of the most powerful forces in the universe," he writes in *The Feeling Good Handbook*. "Self-esteem leads to joy, to productivity, to intimacy." It isn't that difficult to see where the lack of self-esteem takes us.

You might be saying to yourself, "This is all very interesting, but what does self-esteem have to do with business?" To answer this, look back over the history of commerce as we know it today. Six thousand years ago, civilization was based on hunting and gathering; people roamed in small bands scratching out an existence, or at best they lived in marginal villages. When you were born into this culture, you knew, with a very high degree of accuracy, what you would do with your adult life. You might be a hunter, a cook, a gatherer, or a subsistence farmer. You might fish or, if you survived long enough, pass along the collective wisdom of your people. But overall, you probably did not think about your job opportunities, where you might live, or with whom or what group you would spend your adult life. Then, as in much of the underdeveloped world today, your birth determined your identity.

Fast forward to the year 2002. We have gone from the Ice Age through the Stone Age and now to the Information Age—from a hunting to an agrarian to an industrial to a knowledge-driven economy. Today, adult workers commonly make conscious choices about their career, where they live, and whom they choose as associates. All of these seemingly simple decisions require conscious thought. People who do not develop the appropriate skills to make these everyday decisions do not fare well in life—and fare even worse in positions of business leadership. The issue of self-esteem is at the very core of long-term successful leadership.

BACKGROUND

A simple definition of *self-esteem* is the degree to which one does or does not value oneself. Like many terms, however, it means different things depending on who is doing the defining. One of the most important writers on self-esteem is the psychologist Nathaniel Branden.* His book, *The Six Pillars of Self-Esteem,* first introduced this concept to a broad audience. Branden says that self-esteem is what people experience when they demonstrate that they are competent to cope with everyday life. Another essential component of self-esteem, Branden says, is the inner feeling that you, personally, are worthy of and have the right to happiness. The founding fathers of America clearly understood the worth of self-esteem, when they declared in the Bill of Rights that each citizen had the inalienable right to pursue happiness. This statement remains, to this day, one of the most unique and insightful observations about human nature ever placed in a political document.

Self-esteem is both broad and deep. Broad, because it implies the belief that you can handle a variety of challenges; deep, because it is based on a demonstrated ability to handle similar challenges in the past. Ken Osean, an addiction therapist in Dallas, says that many of his young clients come from very wealthy households and already have financial freedom and security. Common among this

---

*For more on self-esteem in the workplace, read Branden's *Self-Esteem at Work* (Jossey-Bass, 1998).

group is an attitude of, "I don't have to do anything because I can do whatever I want." This attitude, he believes, usually comes from parents who have not only provided the financial under-pinnings for such a life but the emotional ones as well by not allowing, or requiring, their children to demonstrate accomplishment. With no opportunity to demonstrate their competence and self-worth, they are highly susceptible to poor self-esteem and addictive behaviors.

This focus on demonstrated ability distinguishes self-esteem from the simple confidence to handle a particular job, or from a confidence that has no basis. Branden identifies six practices, or pillars, as central to the development of his brand of self-esteem. They are:

1. Living consciously

2. Showing self-acceptance

3. Exhibiting self-responsibility

4. Acting self-assertively

5. Living purposefully

6. Practicing personal integrity

These six pillars are not at all odd or esoteric when put into practice. Living consciously calls for you to respect facts, pay attention to what needs attention, and to be open to information, even if it's critical. Self-acceptance means owning up to and taking responsibility for your thoughts, feelings, and actions. Self-responsibility calls on you to avoid blaming other people or circumstances for your choices and actions. Self-assertiveness means standing up for who you are. Living purposefully means choosing and pursuing worthy goals. Personal integrity is telling the truth, honoring commitments, and dealing fairly with others.

Psychologist Albert Ellis is one of the pioneers of a popular and influential branch of psychotherapy called cognitive behavioral therapy, which holds as one of its principles that self-esteem is critical to happiness and efficacy. Ellis considers self-esteem, or *self-worth* as he terms it, so powerful, that he advises people not to monkey around with trying to evaluate their worthiness or lack thereof. "If you rate yourself as having intrinsic worth or value as a human," he and coauthor Robert Harper write in *A Guide to Rational Living*, "you'd better claim to have it by virtue of your mere existence, your aliveness—and not because of anything you do to earn it."

Ancient Underpinnings

The concept of self-esteem extends back to the days when gods were believed to rule the world. Narcissus, one of the earliest heroes of ancient Greek and Roman mythology, exemplified the opposite extreme of low self-esteem. Tales told by the Greek poet Homer in the seventh or eighth century B.C. recount the story of Persephone, a maiden who gathered the fantastically beautiful blooms of the narcissus flower, despite the god Zeus's ban against it. For her transgression, Persephone was kidnapped by the king of the dead and carried forever into the dark underworld.

Nothing quite so dire has been recorded in the annals of business, although not a few corporate boards in the 1980s probably felt like Persephone after attracting the attention of one of that era's ruthless corporate raiders. But the later story of a youth with the same name as the flower, told by the Roman Ovid, is not so far removed from what you may read in the business pages about many a modern enterprise.

Narcissus, we are told, was so beautiful that all women desired him. But Narcissus cruelly turned them away until one of the maidens he had scorned prayed to the gods. "May he who loves not others love himself," she implored, which actually is a lot worse than it sounds. As Narcissus's fate would have it, the righteous god Nemesis heard the prayer and responded forcefully. The next time Narcissus leaned over a pool to drink, he caught sight of his reflection and, smitten by his beauty, refused to turn away for anything. He took neither food nor drink and ultimately died, a victim of Nemesis's righteous wrath.

Narcissus is remembered today as the name of a condition known as narcissism, which is characterized by an exaggerated self-love. The story of Narcissus makes the point that an overweening self-regard can be as dangerous as low self-esteem. They are of course different in practice if not in result. Instead of feeling all criticisms as near-mortal wounds, the narcissist ignores them as irrelevant. Unable to grow, develop, and mature, he follows his own counsel, in love with his own view of things—and in the end often does about as well as the mythical youth.

Sometimes telling the difference between narcissism and hardheadedness is difficult through casual observation. Confident, assertive, determined, able to remove obstacles—all are worthy attributes when used to describe a positive accomplishment. Arrogant, egotistical, aggressive, obsessed, pushy—all are negative terms used to describe a similar failure.

But—make no mistake—while narcissism and a healthy self-esteem may share some similar roots, they are very different in observation. Narcissists have an unrealistic sense of entitlement, for instance. They believe that the normal rules don't apply to them. The real estate and gaming tycoon, Donald Trump, is routinely hailed and punished in the business media as a leader who breaks the rules.

When Donald Trump was on top of the business world, touting his many accomplishments, he was considered both a visionary and great leader. After the near financial collapse of the Trump organizations, the business press routinely attributed his failure to his maniacal self-promotion and arrogance. Did Trump go from a healthy self-esteem to narcissism? Having bounced back yet again, Trump is penning his third book on success, while at the same time fighting creditors over loan defaults. In this regard, Trump is something of an exception to the rule, though the verdict is still out.

In light of evidence to the contrary, narcissists will stay in a fight long after their defeat is obvious to everyone but themselves. Why? Because they cannot accept that their personal perception of truth is not reality. "Chainsaw" Al Dunlop, the ex-CEO of Sunbeam, broadcast his "wonderful" performance and leadership know-how, only to have his selective history of deceit surface after his termination.

Both Trump and "Chainsaw" have publicly demonstrated one of the hallmarks of narcissism—namely that it is all about them. Sure other executives contributed, but narcissists promote themselves as a team of one. They ensure that credit for any positive outcomes flows in their direction.

When employees begin quitting over leadership issues, when customers start complaining about poor attitude, when the firm loses important contacts, when shareholders (especially majority) are ignored, and when boisterous claims of righteousness and entitlement spew from the leaders's lips, get prepared for the inevitable showdown in the executive suite. These precursors are the dark clouds on the distant horizon that mark a storm rapidly approaching.

Although issues of self-esteem tend to surface more in family-managed and closely held enterprises, they can be a stumbling block in public corporations, which are far more often privately managed than publicly controlled. If you work for a business owned or controlled by a family not your own, whether you're the CEO or a first-day clerk, you know that people with their names over the door are in charge. It's a waste of time to pretend that this doesn't matter, and one of the places it matters a great deal is in the development of essential self-esteem among family business heirs.

There's nothing wrong, of course, with family heirs running the show. The key point is whether or not they allow others to develop high self-esteem. An executive who doesn't allow others to grow, no matter their name or affiliation with the people in charge, can fairly be suspected of harboring low self-esteem himself.

It's no secret that members of family businesses are, often, promoted based on their family ties rather than their demonstrated abilities. Promotions may be based on ownership of a sufficient percentage of shares, or the prospect of inheriting them, or even whom they married, but the principle is the same. They get the job because of their relationships, not their talent.

Something similar can occur in any business where a highly placed executive effectively adopts a lower-placed employee, taking a personal interest like a Mafia godfather, mentoring the underling, and eventually identifying with him or her no less than if he were a biological relative. The resulting message to others: talent is not the main criteria for upward movement.

Now, if you are on the receiving end, this might sound like a great situation—you get the job without having to earn it. But it's not as great as it sounds. The experience of being known as a business scion is not one that tends to build self-esteem, no matter how fancy the title, how large the salary, or the extent of the perks.

The business reality is that nepotism—favoritism shown or patronage granted by persons in high office to relatives or close friends—is practiced in almost every closely held business I have encountered and, in many circumstances, is causing varying degrees of damage to the individual rather than the intended positive result.

No matter how counterintuitive it may seem, the practice of nepotism on high-potential leaders is more likely to erode their self-esteem and potential than build it up. It isn't always bad. There's nothing wrong with giving a break to your kids or protégés. If nepotism is connected to real training and the development of real confidence and is used to support and develop self-esteem in the people you have identified as future leaders, it's not a problem. But at some point, those selected must actually perform if they are to develop that essential self-esteem. Nepotism undiluted by a requirement to perform is a dangerous and destructive thing.

Business environments that practice a fast track for friends, family members, or other colleagues do not usually require that these favored individuals earn their titles, salaries, or perks. Those come with the relationship. Few experiences in life build greater self-esteem than earning, through one's efforts, some reward such as financial gain, recognition, or simply a feeling of personal accomplishment. Some scions don't have that experience, because they don't have to exert themselves. The laurel wreath has been handed to them on a platter. With it comes absolutely no sense of accomplishment or personal pride.

Family business executives, in particular, are not filtered for low self-esteem. One much less often finds an executive at the top of a public company who lacks self-esteem, because public companies, in part due to their accountability, function more like meritocracies than family firms. Most senior managers have to earn their positions by effort and accomplishment, and these exertions are powerful self-esteem builders.

In all businesses, the power dynamics inherent within the relationships of people who must work together, especially managers, tend to corrode self-esteem. This is particularly true when the business founder or a heavy-handed dictatorial CEO remains in power. These entrepreneurs tend to be driven, focused, self-confident, and intolerant of others with differing opinions. They may quash any signals of initiative among lower-level employees or offspring, sometimes cruelly. Few acts can be more destructive to self-esteem than such control by the all-powerful head of your family and business.

Easy entry to the executive suite sounds great, hence the saying, "You can marry more money in five minutes than you can earn in a lifetime." So what's wrong with having it soft? The problem, as I have seen time and again, is that not needing to prove themselves means that later-generation business leaders lack the experience in competency that psychologists, such as Branden, have found essential to proper self-esteem. Too often, a future leader who has never worked for or produced results may well conclude that he can't. Who could blame him, in the absence of evidence to the contrary?

ACTION ITEM 1

Require all future leaders to work for what they get. Base promotion, compensation, commendation, and opportunities on measurable performance. You will develop their self-esteem while building company morale and respect for management.

Most jobs are about making money, while other jobs are about gaining the right kind of experience. First jobs can be critical to the long-term development of self-esteem. As a youngster experiencing your first job, almost any role will do.

My first job was as a newspaper delivery boy. I shared this experience with my neighbor, Greg Rohde. Greg and I woke up each morning and, together, wrapped and delivered newspapers throughout our neighborhood. Sunday mornings, we would meet at the Esso station to wrap our papers at 3:00 AM to have them on doorsteps by 6:00. This first job taught me both responsibility and sacrifice. Almost 40 years have passed since Greg and I worked the paper route, and I am proud to say that he started Rohde's, a landscape and nursery business that today is one of the most successful in Dallas, Texas. Greg and I remain the closest of friends.

Many people could overcome the handicap of a rough start in business under the thumb of an esteem-destroying superior by finding a different environment. But in a family business, one cannot escape the instigators of the treatment. The ego-crushing father, mother, sibling, or in-law remains on the scene, often in charge of everyone's life to one degree or another, for many years. Under these circumstances, executives suffering from low self-esteem are distressingly common in family businesses.

To make matters worse, the indecision, poor judgment, and lack of people skills evidenced by many with low self-esteem often lie hidden for many years. Then one day, the CEO retires or dies, and suddenly the ill-prepared manager is thrust into a role for which she is profoundly ill-equipped.

ACTION ITEM 2

Take action now to cope with the eventual departure of your company's current leaders by working to build self-esteem in the next generation of leaders.

Unfortunately, some people in business are narcissistic, especially top executives. They feel their knowledge is superior, their opinions more valid, and their abilities exceptional. In general, these individuals believe they're better than other people and typically harbor an attitude of, "My truth is *the* truth." These individuals usually surround themselves with sycophants unwilling to disagree—the classic "Emperor Has No Clothes" syndrome.

I came across a classic case of this in my consulting work. The son of the founder of a successful West Coast business, now run by a younger brother, received a salary of $1.2 million a year plus an exotic automobile, use of the company jet, and a very liberal entertainment expense account. In exchange, he did little, if any, work. Lacking professional business training and any significant business experience outside the company, he could hardly be expected to earn his exorbitant income. However, the fact that he was the founder's son and the CEO's brother meant—to him at least—that he was better than anyone and everyone else at the company. He was disdainful of all the employees, had a deeply ingrained sense of entitlement, and expected everyone to defer to his opinions.

Excessive pay isn't the only special perquisite granted to members of the inner circle of an enterprise. Executive washrooms, lavishly appointed corner offices, special cafeterias, and even reserved parking spaces can be powerful symbols of superiority over others. For precisely this reason, these symbols are commonly granted to the perceived elite. Unfortunately, the ability of seemingly innocuous extras to create an impression of personal superiority among those who receive them is not benign. They contribute powerfully to the attitude some anointed leaders have, namely that they are better than everybody else.

Leaders are especially susceptible in the circumstances common to growing up in a family business; i.e., everyone defers to you, no one criticizes your decisions, and you watch your parent dominate everyone else. One day, you look on the door, like Narcissus looking into his reflecting pool, and see your name. The next thing you know the telephone rings, and it's Nemesis calling for you.

ACTION ITEM 3

Examine the compensation, benefits, and deference paid to future leaders. It's hard for self-esteem to bloom in a culture of excessive pay, perks, and coddling.

No businessperson wants to depend on material that can't be produced internally or at least sourced from several suppliers. Luckily, self-esteem is not one of them. You can take a number of concrete steps to encourage and cultivate it.

First, however, determine if self-esteem is an issue. Time and energy spent acquiring a commodity your business doesn't need is time and energy wasted. Fortunately, a lack of self-esteem tends to manifest in a handful of highly visible ways. The easily recognized signs of low self-esteem include mannerisms such as a tendency to avoid looking directly at other people and avoiding (in Western societies, at least) a handshake or offering a flabby one. Look at appearance. Do they adopt an exaggeratedly shabby dress?

These signs of low self-esteem are actually among the more subtle. You may also find far more flagrant evidence of serious psychological issues that can, in the worst cases, go far beyond low self-esteem. These include signs or statements indicating suicidal thoughts, gambling addictions, abuse of alcohol or use of illegal drugs, and outbursts of aggressiveness or even outright violence. You may also see indications that a leader is feeling so personally overwhelmed by depression or lack of self-worth, that he is unable to make decisions or function effectively. He may spend long periods alone behind closed doors, for example, while failing to produce significant work.

These behaviors often signal that the individual feels as though she is undeserving of or unqualified for their position in life. While these traits won't necessarily cause trouble by themselves, they are often signs of low self-esteem and a harbinger of trouble to come.

ACTION ITEM 4

Take a careful look around to see whether low self-esteem is an issue among future leaders in your business. It may take several subtle forms that will require some analysis to assess.

Someone else with low self-esteem may appear anxious or fearful, even when circumstances don't warrant it. He may cry easily or appear excessively nervous in most situations. Someone who quickly crumples under any kind of pressure is also likely to suffer from low self-esteem. Occasionally, such people have so little self-esteem that they are willing, even eager, to shoulder the guilt for events in which they had no part.

Perversely, low self-esteem can go hand in hand with the opposite tendency, to become aggressively offended even in relatively inoffensive situations. The person with low self-esteem feels threatened, even when the actual threat is minimal or nonexistent. If your business has a manager who seems unable to take even well-intentioned criticism, someone who reacts very defensively to any negative comment, or who works overtime to deflect blame for missteps elsewhere, low self-esteem may be at work.

Self-esteem issues may also be camouflaged. Some people with low self-esteem actually appear overly confident. This seeming paradox is a sham. Their attitude is a façade erected to ward off threats and probes. Loud, blustery personalities often conceal self-esteem shortfalls. They commonly manifest among offspring of successful business founders who are urged to display qualities of leadership and bravado, despite feeling the opposite.

When all else fails, you can simply ask a person you suspect of suffering from low self-esteem how she feels. People who are frequently or constantly sad, discouraged, unmotivated, and troubled by feelings of inferiority, guilt, or indecisiveness can often trace their situation to low self-esteem.

ACTION ITEM 5

One of the greatest sources of learning is failure. Among other things, it lets us see the reality of those around us as well as ourselves. Although many people project a tough, competent image, when confronted with a painful failure, they can crumble.

To improve or encourage the development of self-esteem, give people opportunities to prove themselves. Provide them with real tasks with real responsibilities. Smiley faces, false praise, and group awards do not develop an individual's self-esteem. People must be held accountable and their tasks be of real significance. Only actual accomplishment can build self-esteem.

PORTRAIT OF SUCCESS

Richard Wackenhut

The path from a job as a security guard to president and chief executive of a 75,000-person company is long and not particularly easy. But Richard R. Wackenhut took this path with the blessing of his father, George R. Wackenhut. The senior Wackenhut was an ex-FBI agent when he started Wackenhut Corporation in 1953. As the company grew, his son worked his way up through various positions—investigator, salesperson, manager, and, beginning in 1986, CEO.

Today, Wackenhut, in Palm Beach Gardens, Florida, is one of the country's largest independent providers of security services, doing everything from guarding American embassies overseas to protecting nuclear plants and providing security for private prisons. The CEO's broad experience in the field has helped him negotiate intense competition that virtually drove the firm out of the airport security business, as well as a prison scandal involving allegations of inmate abuse by Wackenhut employees.

These experiences with failure, as well as success, have helped Richard Wackenhut not only navigate tough times but also not to be overimpressed by the promise of easy profits. In the wake of the September 11, 2001, terrorist attacks in the United States, Wackenhut suddenly began receiving large volumes of inquiries from current, former, and prospective customers who wanted help with security, screening, identification, and other issues related to preventing terrorism.

Another executive with less experience might have gone overboard trying to meet the sudden upsurge in demand. But Richard Wackenhut's many years working at all levels in the company provided him with invaluable perception, leading to skepticism about what all the activity would mean to his firm.

"We're getting a lot of calls and a lot of increased work," he was quoted as saying shortly after the attacks. "Whether that's short term or long term remains to be seen."

You should not expect someone with low self-esteem to function like a champion simply because you have posed a challenge. Leave nothing to chance. Catastrophic failure at a challenge may do more harm than good. Therefore, structure learning opportunities so that failure is not very likely or at least, in the event failure does occur, the company isn't seriously damaged. The idea is that by proving themselves competent, people become more competent. The point is not to set someone up for failure or to harm the company in the process.

When establishing a plan to build self-esteem in an employee, think small. It does almost no good to assign a big challenge and then review it one year later. Start by breaking the business challenge into smaller pieces, and recognize the progress as it unfolds. Create a challenge that has lots and lots of "little wins" to keep interest and enthusiasm high.

For example, one common and effective technique is to assign a person to open a new office, study a new market, or head up a new division. The newness of these situations makes it harder for low self-esteem sufferers to be judged harshly, by themselves or others, because they can't be compared against prior results. You wouldn't, on the other hand, assign someone with shaky self-esteem to follow up an assignment behind one of your star performers. New offices, markets, and divisions should be chosen so that success or failure is not critical to the company's success. You're trying to build self-esteem, not create a threat to the company.

Critical to long-term success is embracing the attitude that everybody must work her way up the totem pole. Nothing could be a bigger mistake than to take an untested youth and thrust him into the top job. Not only will you foster resentment and mistrust among other members of the organization, but it won't do the youth, who probably knows only too well that he doesn't belong in the job, any good either.

Better to start a protégé off at a low level and then, by a gradual series of promotions, move them into the level that their interests and abilities indicate. I have known many future leaders who start out by sweeping up the warehouse, then move into a clerical position in the administrative offices, then into various jobs in the marketing, finance, operations, and other departments. A one-year or two-year stint in each major functional unit is a good idea. The main point is: let them go out and experience the real world, storms and all, but keep close at hand and protect them from catastrophic failure.

In the case of a seasoned senior executive who joins the enterprise after years of relevant successful experience, take advantage of the opportunity to test their skills early on by having them spend time in several areas of the company. Not only will this experience build their knowledge more quickly, but this simple demonstration will alert employees that they have a hands-on boss.

My uncles' foresight and steady hand guided me in this approach very successfully. The experience and confidence that I gained from working as a commission-based telemarketer for two years, then moving into photography and sales, was invaluable. At each step, I was measured against other employees throughout the company and compensated on standard incentive pay. My work performance was paid the same as for any other employee. Others saw how I was compensated, and thus fairness was never a barrier to good working relationships. This approach gave me the deep confidence to understand and eventually teach others how to perform and achieve performance goals. Years later, when I was managing operations for Olan Mills Studios, no one ever doubted that I understood field operations.

This exposure came in very handy when in 1992 and 1993, I needed to restructure several divisions that had grown too fast. I ended up personally removing 25 percent of the field management.

Removing long-time employees, many of whom are very loyal and dedicated, is never easy. But armed with firsthand experience and an intimate understanding of their respective positions, I was able to act without unusually harsh criticism, or any lawsuits, claims, or settlements. I attribute this success in large part to the widespread belief that I was a hands-on manager, current with how the business operated. I was one of them, not a disinterested or disconnected third party, removed from the day-to day consequences.

A stair-step approach will present future leaders with increasingly significant challenges which, when mastered, will provide a boost to self-esteem. It also provides young workers with a good feel for the overall company, and as a side benefit lets them test numerous jobs to see where they fit best.

So far, the business leader sounds like sort of a managerial Jim Henson, jerking strings here and inserting a hand there to supply pseudochallenges and predetermined promotions. Sure, some planning and a little manipulation are probably required, but being told what to do, with no opportunity to decide your own fate, is not conducive to developing robust self-esteem.

So give future leaders choices. Let them decide what area of the company interests them. If it is sales, when operations was always your love, so be it. Swallow your disappointment, and let them do it their way. If they want to do something else for a few years before joining the company, control your impatience. The rewards you'll get in the way of a more mature, balanced, and grounded businessperson will be worth it.

It's hard to start your concern for self-esteem too early. When I took my two sons out for our regular father-son dinners, I let them choose the place we would eat. This may sound like a small sacrifice but, after all, how many pizzas can I eat? The cost of a few extra servings of fast food was worth it in exchange for watching them balance the competing attractions of burgers and fries against sausage and pepperoni. The fact that they couldn't have both and therefore had to choose meant they were learning, even if in a sim-

plistic way, about opportunity costs and the basics of making decisions. It also meant that in this choice, at least, they were the boss.

When the stakes are larger than dinner, letting young wings fly
on their own is not as easy. What if, as in many business builders's
worst nightmares, the next generation in the business decides not
to be the next generation in that business, or perhaps in any business? They become afflicted with the dreaded "Harley over Har-
vard Syndrome."

The best advice is to accept the decision as calmly as possible.
People change their minds, especially when they find out that
working as, say, an actor isn't as great as they thought. Many a wan-
dering businessperson has returned to the fold after an adventure
or two in another field. We have certainly seen this in abundance
recently, as powerful business leaders left their secure industry
positions to tackle the challenges of a dot-com opportunity, only to
return en masse during 2001.

ACTION ITEM 6

*Part of building self-esteem is making your own decisions and living
by them. People can't do this if you make their decisions for them. So,
let potential leaders choose their own path if at all feasible. They may
not choose the one you want, but they and you will be better if it's truly
the one they want.*

Encouraging career exploration and freedom is very difficult
and often challenges the corporate culture. Whether they know it
or not, most CEOs have a grand scheme about where things should
go and how the company should operate. It is one reason why they
usually try to control every facet of the business. These individuals
need unbiased feedback. Too often, managers who are seen by the
rank and file as favored by higher-ups are treated—overtly, at
least—as founts of infallible wisdom. Any comment or suggestion

they make, no matter how eye-rollingly foolish, is implemented as soon as possible.

The problem, of course, is that people eventually have to operate in the real world, where their suggestions will be treated as just that and their ideas will succeed or fail based on merit. Now is the time to get them used to impartial feedback. Otherwise, they won't know a good idea from a bad one, or how to challenge a dangerous but superficially attractive proposal.

The difficulty is that somebody has to provide the feedback. In many companies, insiders are simply unwilling, out of fear or respect or duty, to speak plainly to those in the inner circle of decision makers. Their reluctance is understandable. Not a few employees have been summarily discharged for failing to show a seemly respect to a member of the ruling clique. Even if the member in question is a junior associate at the moment, it's possible or even likely that someday he will be the boss. And frankly, input contrary to a course of action favored by management isn't welcome in far too many companies. Employees know that and keep their mouths shut.

After working with a wide variety of businesses and their most senior leaders, I am now generally able to assess the degree of self-esteem among a firm's leadership by testing and observing how open they are to feedback. If the firm's culture does not allow dissent and feedback, then generally this culture is closed and not open to learning. Leaders with lower self-esteem usually are at the top of these closed cultures.

Conversely, in organizations that are defined through the free flow of information and communication up and down the organization, you are likely to find leaders who are emotionally mature, eager to learn, and open to candid feedback. The presence of strong self-esteem turns the company into a learning organization.

ACTION ITEM 7

Scrutinize feedback to make sure that it is honest, direct, credible, and helpful. You don't do anyone a favor by pulling punches when it comes to fairly criticizing the performance of up-and-comers working in the business, especially when they are family members.

Changing widespread, deeply held attitudes is difficult, especially in companies with a large number of employees. An effective approach is to designate one employee, perhaps a long-time retainer, to provide unvarnished feedback to developing protégés. Make it clear that speaking the unpleasant truth will not endanger this employee's livelihood.

This can work even in the smallest firms. One four-person mechanical engineering company I know of consisted of the father, his son, and two unrelated employees. Relations between the father and son were cordial, but because of the son's simmering desire to pursue a career in the military rather than in civil engineering, less than ideal.

The father found it difficult to criticize his son, for fear of unleashing repressed frustration and driving him away. Believing that honest feedback would be taken as criticism and hurt his child's self-esteem (the exact opposite is true), he sought assistance from the other employees. One of the nonfamily workers was, while experienced, far junior in the hierarchy to the son and unwilling to offer anything other than instant obedience and meaningless acquiescence. The father asked the other nonfamily employee, who was also experienced but far more trusted due to a long relationship with the father, to mentor the young son. This employee had the confidence and the spoken assent of the father to offer plain comments. As a result, the son felt comfortable enough to stay in the firm, and he pursued his military career part-time as a reservist.

ACTION ITEM 8

Pick a trusted employee of the business to serve as an honest sounding board and mentor for rising stars. Protect this person from backlash.

Boxes and barrels of self-esteem aren't going to solve all problems. Many, if not most, business woes are caused by factors beyond immediate direct control—the loss of a key customer, a shift in market needs, a change in government regulations, or maybe even an act of war. A Wal-Mart going in down the road has spelled doom for many small retailers who weren't conceivably at fault in their business plan.

You can have too much self-esteem, too. Some narcissistic people really do think they're the greatest. They can, with their grandiose, self-important ways, cause as much or more trouble than an indecisive, irrelevant sufferer from poor self-esteem. Unfortunately, it's easier to build up someone's self-esteem than to take someone down a notch without risking some damaging confrontations along the way.

The upshot is that you need to recognize that some people will have unfixable self-esteem problems. These people need to be eased out of key positions and critical operations as gracefully as possible, whether by presenting them with an attractive severance package, assignment to a sleepy office or a dead-end project, or relocation to a no-growth branch.

But solid self-esteem helps in tangible ways. For one thing, it will improve decision making. A key trait of people with appropriate levels of self-esteem is that they can confront reality unflinchingly—at least as well as any of us is able. From this perspective, they can make decisions with superior outcomes.

By comparison, a decision maker with low self-esteem is likely to base a selection on information that, while feeling comfortable, may be inaccurate. For instance, an executive lacking self-esteem, when faced with market data suggesting a new product will fail, is likely to ignore that data if he has much at stake in the development project. This is precisely how poor self-esteem leads to poor business performances. A leader who fears change is not a champion for progress.

Appropriate self-esteem helps in other areas as well. Someone who properly regards her own worth will also value other people correctly. Being able to assess others and, equally important, to convey the impression that you value others accurately, is of immeasurable importance in establishing the close relationships with suppliers, customers, and employees that are of great worth to a business.

Finally, and perhaps most importantly, a solid sense of self-esteem helps people bounce back from inevitable failure. It's no secret that many notable successes in all spheres of life have been preceded by notable failures. Abraham Lincoln's record of losing political races and failing at business is almost more impressive than his eventual success as perhaps America's greatest President. A high school dropout named Johnnie Hunt failed so miserably at his first effort to start a company that he had to go back to work for somebody else for more than a decade before he started another. But that firm would become J.B. Hunt Transport, one of the country's largest truck lines and a wealth generator that made Hunt one of only nine high school dropouts on the Forbes 400 list of the richest Americans. Self-esteem is the only fuel that can power that kind of determination.

You have your pick of attitudes toward self-esteem—reject it, laugh about it, insist like Groucho Marx that you wouldn't be a member of any club that would have you. But when the people you're going to count on to carry on your enterprise show a glimmer of it, don't serve yourself some more potatoes and then laugh them under the table. Let them be themselves, and they'll have a better chance of being like you. Maybe someday people will wonder about your protégé, "Where did Johnny learn to work so well?"

ACTION ITEMS

ACTION ITEM 1

Require all future leaders to work for what they get. Base promotion, compensation, commendation, and opportunities on measurable performance. You will develop their self-esteem while building company morale and respect for management.

ACTION ITEM 2

Take action now to cope with the eventual departure of your company's current leaders by working to build self-esteem in the next generation of leaders.

ACTION ITEM 3

Examine the compensation, benefits, and deference paid to future leaders. It's hard for self-esteem to bloom in a culture of excessive pay, perks, and coddling.

ACTION ITEM 4

Take a careful look around to see whether low self-esteem is an issue among future leaders in your business. It may take several subtle forms that will require some analysis to assess.

ACTION ITEM 5

One of the greatest sources of learning is failure. Among other things, it lets us see the reality of those around us as well as ourselves. Although many people project a tough, competent image, when confronted with a painful failure, they can crumble.

ACTION ITEM 6

Part of building self-esteem is making your own decisions and living by them. People can't do this if you make their decisions for them. So, let potential leaders choose their own path. They may not choose the one you want, but they and you will be better if it's truly the one they want.

ACTION ITEM 7

Scrutinize feedback to make sure that it is honest, direct, credible, and helpful. You don't do anyone a favor by pulling your punches when it comes to criticizing the performance of up-and-comers working in the business.

ACTION ITEM 8

Pick a trusted employee of the business to serve as an honest sounding board and mentor for rising stars. Protect this person from backlash.

CHAPTER 2

Make It a Meritocracy

Thanks, Mom. When I landed my first job in the business where I would spend most of my career, the thought that crossed my mind was not, "I deserve this," but, "Thanks, Mom." Given that I showed up late, out of breath, dirty, and soaked with perspiration after my 12-year-old car died in a busy intersection during the rush-hour heat of a Phoenix summer, I might well have been turned away from my first day of work—but for the fact that my mother was Olan Mills's daughter.

As it turned out, I rose to the top ranks of Olan Mills's executives—at least in part through merit, I like to think. But you can't count on such benign outcomes from automatically hiring and promoting employees merely, or mainly, because they belong to the right family, went to the right college, belong to the right ethnic group, or otherwise conform to some characteristic not related to merit. Businesses that fail to follow principles for creating effective meritocracies shouldn't expect to build a culture of sustainable success.

Making a business a true meritocracy isn't easy or, in its pristine definition, even possible. It is not as simple as merely saying "no" to the automatic hiring and promotion of grandchildren of the founder, unfortunately. Meritocracy is sabotaged by many factors other than genetic relation. Companies that hire and promote executives based entirely or partly on their gender, religion, ethnic background, age, or educational background are doing the same thing. To create a meritocracy, you have to be aware of preferential treatment in hiring, performance appraisals, promotions, and assignments, and stamp it out like the plague for the long-range good of the enterprise.

WHY PEOPLE IGNORE MERIT

Family ties provide the most common and most troublesome basis for ignoring merit in hiring, compensating, and promoting people. If you're the owner or the CEO of a company, you may well find yourself in a position to help out your son, daughter, or other relation. Barring antinepotism rules at your company, there's no reason why you shouldn't. The world is full of successful firms run by people whose primary claim to a corner office is having the same last name as the company's founder. For an example, you don't have to look any further than Ford Motor Co. In 1999, William Clay Ford, Jr., referred to as Bill, was named chairman of the company his great-grandfather Henry Ford had founded 97 years earlier. In 2001, after the family ownership block lost confidence in Jacques Nasser, Bill assumed additional responsibilities as CEO. One of the key issues that contributed to Nasser's termination (officially a resignation) were lawsuits filed by aggrieved Ford employees, challenging Nasser's salaried employee review policy as discriminatory—nonmeritocratic. Since then, Ford hasn't done badly, solidifying its position as the world's second-largest car company (and the largest pickup truck maker), as well as America's largest auto finance company and the world's leading car rental firm. Despite being publicly traded, Ford is still in many respects a family firm, the Ford family owning about 40 percent of the voting stock.

Educational background is another frequent source of favoritism. So you have an Ivy League degree. The Ivies have illustrious reputations for their educational quality, and discerning organizations. Firms, especially those based in the Northeast, favored hiring their graduates. Some enterprises go so far as to prefer graduates of one particular college to another. The Central Intelligence Agency, for example, is reportedly dominated by Yale University alumni who prefer to hire people who also graduated from the New Haven campus. But ivy on the walls isn't the only qualification that can be subject to discrimination. For many years, General Motors Corp. displayed favoritism to graduates of Midwestern universities, specifically those within the Big 10 Conference. Sometimes there are good reasons for favoring people from one educational background or university. People who went to school together naturally find it easier to form teams, and often graduates feel security surrounded by like people. It also helps with alumni fund raising.

Ethnicity has proven to be one of the forms of discrimination that is most widespread and difficult to eradicate. Serious modern American efforts to end this type of discrimination date back to at least the Civil Rights Act of 1964, which prohibits employment discrimination based on race, color, religion, sex, or national origin. Despite many years of civil rights activism through social reform, advancement of minority leadership, enforcement of the 1964 Act, and enactment of other antidiscrimination legislation, discrimination based on race, color, and country of national origin remains widespread in the United States and many other countries. At any given time, the Federal Bureau of Investigation's Office of Equal Employment Opportunity Affairs, which is responsible for investigating all matters of discrimination in the workplace, is working on hundreds of open cases alleging various forms of employment-related discrimination. Many more cases, of course, never come to the FBI's attention because the people subject to discrimination are unwilling or afraid to report the problem. Again, humans seem to have strong desires to work with others that share similar backgrounds.

Hiring and promoting on the basis of gender—most often males—is one of the activities forbidden by the 1964 Civil Rights Act in the United States and by similar laws in many other countries. Yet it, too, occurs frequently. Many working women silently accept the "glass ceiling" concept. In industry after industry, females represent approximately 50 percent of the workforce but are represented as a small percentage of management. When the concentration of women into a few functions, such as human resources and public relations, is taken into account, the glass ceiling in areas such as finance and operations becomes even lower and, seemingly, more impenetrable.

Most forms of discrimination based on racial or ethnic background or country of origin are against the law in the United States and many other countries. In many companies, the hiring of people related to current employees is frowned upon if not actually proscribed by company policy. Why? When you fail to hire and promote as a meritocracy, your company may be headed for serious trouble.

RISKS OF FAILING TO RUN A MERITOCRACY

The risks of instantly hiring and promoting certain employees are numerous. Whether you are favoring people because of the college they attended, their last name, or any other reason not strictly related to merit, you are setting yourself up for some potentially devastating problems.

One of the biggest problems is difficulty recruiting talented outsiders in the future. Today, no company can afford to limit the pool of talent from which it can draw, unless imposing that limitation offers an overriding positive benefit. When current and prospective employees learn—and learn they will, no matter how well the secret is kept—that only "certain types" of people can hope for advancement in an enterprise, only those who fit the mold will even bother to apply for jobs. If hired, they may not stay with you for long. There is no way to calculate the cost of not selecting the best leaders from the employment pool, but whatever it is, it's significant. Businesses simply cannot afford to drive away talented outsiders who fear discrimination if they wish to build long-lasting success.

A diverse workforce is frequently cited as a benefit in its own right. It is a reality within many of the leading firms throughout the United States. After the devastation of the World Trade Center on September 11, 2001, Reuters news service reported that almost one-half of the people killed or reported missing were from foreign nations or were employees of non-U.S. origin. Although this high percentage of diversity does not parallel "Main Street" America, it is a sharp example that leading firms, with a global ambition, adhere to the strengths of diversity. For these and many other leading firms, diversity is much more than an altruistic gesture.

Diversity has some supremely practical benefits that you may sacrifice, if you drive away people who fail to fit a narrow definition of employable, promotable workers. To begin with, a homogeneous workforce is likely to suffer from an impoverished imagination. Without outside viewpoints to draw on, your company is likely to produce uninspired products and generate stale business ideas. Hybrid vigor, the creativity that evolves from mixing different genetic backgrounds, creates offspring who are stronger than either parent. This applies to businesses as well as biology. When you mix up people from varying backgrounds and lead your firm as a true meritocracy, the end result will be more varied and better ideas.

Having a more diverse group of people in your leadership office also gives you more flexibility. For example, if all your senior executives are white, Protestant, middle-aged family men, odds of getting anyone to volunteer to work on Christmas Day are slim to none. Add a few people of other faiths or young men or women without family responsibilities, and your holiday staffing rotations may be easily solved. Flexibility also comes into play in potentially more significant circumstances concerning communication and innovation. For instance, when everyone in leadership at the company comes from the same family, the same school, or the same ethnic group, they will almost certainly receive the same cultural messages. This adds up to being out of touch. If you view the world through narrow slits, you will miss out on many trends that could provide growth opportunities for your business. If, on the other hand, you recruit, develop, and promote people of diverse backgrounds, the firm is better positioned to be more in touch with what is going on in a broader spectrum of societies. Everyone will know what's going on, and you'll be able to use that knowledge to spur long-lasting profitability.

Discrimination lawsuits are also an important reason to make your company a meritocracy. Texaco, now ChevronTexaco Corporation, found this out the hard way a few years back, when it was ordered to pay $176 million in one of the largest racial discrimination lawsuits in U.S. history. The initiating evidence in the case was a tape recording of executives using racial slurs and uttering racist remarks at a company meeting. Texaco is far from the only company guilty of this behavior.

CREATING AN EFFECTIVE MERITOCRACY

To create an effective meritocracy, you first must remove the obstacles to its creation. That means to dismantle the Good Old Boy Club (GOB) that oversees many organizations and, to some extent, is probably influencing yours. The Good Old Boy Club, just to clarify, doesn't have to consist of a bunch of pot-bellied country folk standing around a pickup truck planning how to keep city folk from crashing their game of dominoes. Picture, for example, a group of very sophisticated and high-achieving business leaders in an oak-paneled conference room. They may be discussing, in coded terms, techniques for encouraging a hard-charging female executive to leave the firm so they don't have to promote her to share their privileges. While more subtle, this type of GOB can be very disadvantageous to any business leader endeavoring to create lasting wealth.

Dismantling the GOB is largely a matter of identifying and disrupting it. Once it begins to fall apart, a GOB will disintegrate of its own weight. If you spot a trend of promising leaders reaching a certain point in your organization and then departing the company or languishing and seeming to lose their fire, suspect a GOB is in operation. Likewise, if you just notice a certain sameness in the occupants of the executive suites, odds are this didn't happen by accident. It's probably evidence of GOB controlling the hiring and promotion process for their own purposes.

You can deal with this destructive network by transferring, reassigning or, if necessary, demoting or even firing some of its members. Because GOB networks can definitely be destructive to a company's future prospects, such actions are often easily justifiable. But why deal with poor managers using such crude techniques? Better yet, explain the situation to the managers involved and encourage their participation in the remaking of your company as one free of cronyism. It can be done. Today, it's worth noting, Denny's is lauded as an example of a company that learned its lesson and become a model of tolerance for people of varying racial backgrounds. Let's hope you can accomplish the same thing — without such a costly punishment.

ACTION ITEM 1

Identify and dismantle the networks of cronies in your company for the good of the firm and of those talented leaders who won't want to work for you if you don't.

Reward for Results

In one of the many public interviews granted after the release of his book, *Jack: Straight from the Gut*, Jack Welsh was asked to define his single biggest success while leading General Electric. He replied, "Building a meritocracy. Don't [let] anyone think you are being kind because you give kind appraisals. Business schools should teach more about the dangers of false appraisals. It is one of the most common forms of cruelty."

Appraising performance fairly, for all levels of employees—including the most senior level leaders—is a critical factor for success and should include a discussion of compensation, a thorny issue in almost any enterprise. In fact, in closely held firms, it is one of the top two reasons for ownership conflict. Who gets paid what and why is important, personal, and all too often poorly explained—or even misunderstood by those making compensation decisions. The most effective way to use compensation as a tool for building long-term profitability is: Reward for results. Set objectives for personal performance and for division or company performance. Then compensate based on whether and how participants achieve results. It's that simple.

Simple to state, maybe. Not simple to do. Anyone who has ever tried to design, implement, and manage a commission scheme for salespeople knows that, even in such a seemingly perfect meritocracy where you only get paid for what you sell, ambiguity and arbitrariness inevitably prevail. Arguments will occur and tempers will flare over issues such as who is assigned the most profitable territory, how the credit and commissions are divided on a particular sale that involved two salespeople, and what the cutoff will be for inclusion on this year's President's Round Table or equivalent.

This is why I have personally experimented with or been an advisor to over 100 different compensation methods. All have had merit; none have been perfect. I was the sole author of a particular incentive compensation structure for midlevel and senior managers while I was with Olan Mills, Inc. I thought for sure that I had discovered the compensation equivalent of Cortez's "Seven Cities of Gold." Within nine months, I scrapped my revolutionary approach and returned, on a temporary basis, to rewarding performance arbitrarily.

Compensation encompasses a very broad range of possibilities. For example, how stock options, health and life insurance benefits, use of a company car, or planes, boats, ranches, vacation condos, tickets to ball games, symphony, or society events are managed can determine if compensation will cause an undercurrent of dissatisfaction or be an appreciated perk and reward. In many closely held businesses, senior management and owners will draw an unfairly high salary plus bonus, while other equal owners in nonsenior management positions are paid fair market value for their work. This discrepancy causes very serious problems for owners and managers in forming trusting relationships. To avoid a breakdown of compensation meritocracy, follow the compensation rule: pay all employees a fair market salary, provide an incentive, and then add a bonus for outstanding performance.

Ultimately, I learned. The first part of the compensation riddle is to be as specific as possible when setting the goals on which rewards will be based. Be sure to state precisely how an individual will be measured as well as what their objective should be. For instance, if you are asking a leader to increase profits of a division by a certain percentage, make sure you have a timeline in mind, giving a date when the improvement is supposed to occur. Create lots of small steps and give lots of feedback instead of establishing only one goal that is measured only at the end of the year.

It is also a good idea, when politically palatable, to have an environment that supports open communication about compensation, where salary and incentive ranges are not only known but the logic behind the method is understood by all. While such a system may be uncomfortable for some people—possibly including you—it has the advantage of dispelling rumors about who is making what and why. In the clear light of day, in an open environment, you will find yourself no longer required to justify and defend pay decisions. The result will move your firm one step closer to a pure meritocracy. The single most important guiding principle for establishing compensation to enhance morale and effort (rather than demoralizing the workforce) is to keep whatever formula you use simple and fair.

ACTION ITEM 2

The most effective way to use compensation as a tool for building long-term profitability is simple: Reward for results. Set objectives for leaders to meet, and compensate them based on whether and how they achieve those results.

Promote High Performers

When someone does extremely well at a certain level, the expected outcome is a promotion to the next level. That's true when the raise in level is a simple elevation of existing responsibility, as when a local manager is promoted to become a regional director. It's also true when the change means substantially new duties, such as when a successful sales executive is moved into marketing. This kind of performance-based promotion system is essential if you are to create a true meritocracy. But it doesn't happen by itself. To be sure you're promoting high performers, you must have ways of identifying the top performers in your organization, evaluating them for advancement, and then effectively promoting them.

Identifying top performers is usually a matter of using the information you already have. Comparing sales records, measuring relative performance on cost-cutting initiatives, and the like are second nature to many business managers. But when you do it with an eye to identifying people for possible advancement, you have to do it somewhat differently. To accurately spot future leaders, look for the reasons for good performance. Leaders who overcome adversity, obtain excellent results with average resources, and are able to generate turnaround results are likely to create long-term, profitable track records.

Evaluating for advancement is another matter. Not everyone who does well at one level should advance to the next. The Peter Principle, although arguably overly simplistic, can apply here and is especially troublesome in very small firms and some family businesses, where the likely candidate pool for promotion may include only one or two people. Good performance, however, is one method to identify potential candidates for promotion. Before you can actually advance a candidate, however, you have to compare her skills and talents with the needs of the position you are trying to fill. You may conclude that this person, while performing very well now, won't do well at a higher level—and may not even want higher responsibilities.

ACTION ITEM 3

Be very clear about your firm's long-range objectives when choosing key players for important assignments. "Big picture" issues may justify a divergence from meritocracy.

Football is king in Highland Park, Texas, the Dallas enclave where I live. The National Football League's Dallas Cowboys have achieved the status of legend among most of my neighbors. Before the Cowboys, it was the Southern Methodist University Mustangs, now of the collegiate Western Athletic Conference. The lore of Doak Walker, "Dandy" Don Meredith, Kyle Rote, and Eric Dickerson has been growing in the minds of fans dating back to 1911. The local high school team, the Highland Park Scots, is a perennial contender for the hotly contested Texas high school football championship trophy.

In this environment, it's tough to be a diehard basketball fan. But I am one, so I follow the NBA's Dallas Mavericks. Like all teams, the Mavs have not always chosen the best available players for their roster. Sometimes they learn from their mistakes, and sometimes they don't. The experience of Dennis Rodman stands out as instructive, especially on the point that sometimes a meritocratic system needs close examination to assure that it is considering the proper merits. The characteristics that make a team, a player, a business, or a leader successful may change over time and in different circumstances. Last season's star may be next season's goat.

OUT OF FOCUS

Dennis Rodman

Unquestionably, Dennis Rodman is one of the greatest rebounder and defensive players of his era in the NBA. The Dallas-raised player, nicknamed "The Worm" for his wriggling, energetic style of play, was named to the NBA All-Defensive Team eight years running, starting in 1988. He holds the all-time record for the number of consecutive seasons leading the league in rebounds at seven, beating out even the redoubtable Wilt Chamberlain and Bill Russell for that honor. His teams did all right too. Rodman earned five championship rings during his stints with the Detroit Pistons and the Chicago Bulls.

Yet Dennis was shuffled around to many different teams, primarily because of his attitude. The issue involved more than his flamboyant hair coloring, tattoos, body piercing, and cross-dressing. Rodman was a divisive, disruptive force on every team featuring a less charismatic leader than Michael Jordan or the Piston's Isaiah Thomas. The San Antonio Spurs were more than happy to trade him to Chicago for that reason. After the Bulls disbanded their championship nucleus, Rodman wound up playing for the Mavericks. Coach Don Nelson and owner Mark Cuban believed Rodman's experience and talent would lead them to victory.

But Rodman repeatedly failed to show up for practices and team meetings. Although fined for his antics, he was not deterred. When he got into the games, he put up good numbers, but the team didn't come together and had a losing record with him. In the middle of the season, Rodman was released, with Cuban agreeing to pay him the balance of his contract.

Almost at that moment, the Mavericks came together and started winning games. The point is, despite his stellar playing abilities, his disrespectful, disruptive behavior had a huge negative influence on the team. Did Cuban make a mistake by hiring and then firing him? Not necessarily. It just took time for he and Nelson to realize that in the meritocracy of professional sports, there's more to it than just having a nose for the ball.

Similar situations can occur in a company. Sometimes the best trained, most likely candidate isn't the one to be leading the company at a particular time. When such a candidate is passed over, people may not understand that the decision is based on merit. But what's happening is that the requirements of the job have changed, so the definition of merit has changed. I always think of Dennis Rodman when I see a situation like this developing. It helps me keep an open mind to the possibility that the all-star candidate might not be the wisest choice.

Developing people for advancement is the next step. Too often, leaders are thrust into challenging new assignments without adequate preparation. As a result, they may burn out and leave the organization. If that happens, you have lost out twice. You lose once by mistakenly promoting someone out of a job in which he was doing well, and you lose again by failing to provide additional training or support so the person could do well in the new job.

ACTION ITEM 4

To be sure you're promoting high performers, develop methods of identifying the top performers in your organization and evaluate them for advancement.

Recruit for Diversity

Your business can't become diverse overnight. You have to make diversity come to you. That means hiring people with different educational backgrounds, ethnic groups, gender, and other diverse characteristics. Unless your company already has a reputation as a place where people of diverse backgrounds are welcome and given an equal chance to succeed, you have to look for these people and make an offer that's attractive to them.

ACTION ITEM 5

Your business can't become diverse overnight. You have to make diversity come to you. That means you have to look for the people who will make your organization a diverse meritocracy and make an offer that's attractive to them.

Help High Performers Join In

High performers, it stands to reason, ought to have no trouble conforming to the culture of your company. In this case, however, reason is suspect. The fact is, many people who are excellent leaders and managers need a little assistance when it comes to joining the upper ranks. Given that you should value leaders based on their ability to lead, it only makes sense that you should help promising up-and-comers with the niceties of society, so they can remain with your organization and lead it effectively.

Golf provides a perfect example of what I'm talking about. Discussing business on the links is an age-old tradition in business. Many deals have been struck and relationships begun among members of a foursome playing a leisurely 18 holes. Golf is so important an aspect of doing business in many companies and industries, that those otherwise able leaders who don't practice the game will find themselves at a disadvantage. Chief among these handicapped leaders are women executives. This is true for several reasons. For one thing, fewer women play golf—female golfers make up just 19 percent of the U.S. golfing population. For another, golf is an athletic endeavor based on physical abilities that tend to differ between sexes—men and women tee off from different spots on the course. Finally, golf isn't just a sport. It's a culture with rules regarding when you can talk, how long you can take to make a shot, and where you should stand while someone else is putting. Women who haven't played much and don't understand all the unspoken rules and etiquette aren't likely to be invited on many golf outings, no matter how open-minded the company's other executives are. That's why an increasing number of companies are actually teaching their female leaders to play golf. It's a way to make their female executives better businesspeople, while helping their companies at the same time.

ACTION ITEM 6

Don't assume that people with promising abilities will naturally rise to the top of your corporate culture. Instead, work to help promising up-and-comers with the niceties of business mores and protocol, so they can remain with your organization and lead it effectively.

The phenomenon of teaching golf to some executives provides a good example of how to make a business a true meritocracy. At the same time, it offers an explanation of why those fortunate, golf-savvy female executives may, from time to time, sigh and say, "Thanks, Dad, for helping me learn to play golf."

ACTION ITEMS

ACTION ITEM 1

Identify and dismantle the networks of cronies in your company for the good of the firm and of those talented leaders who won't want to work for you if you don't.

ACTION ITEM 2

The most effective way to use compensation as a tool for building long-term profitability is simple. Reward for results. Set objectives for leaders to meet, and compensate them based on whether and how they achieve those results.

ACTION ITEM 3

Be very clear about your firm's long-range objectives when choosing key players for important assignments. "Big picture" issues may justify a divergence from meritocracy.

ACTION ITEM 4

To be sure you're promoting high performers, develop methods of identifying the top performers in your organization and evaluate them for advancement.

ACTION ITEM 5

Your business can't become diverse overnight. You have to make diversity come to you. That means you have to look for the people who will make your organization a diverse meritocracy and make an offer that's attractive to them.

ACTION ITEM 6

Don't assume that people with promising abilities will naturally rise to the top of your corporate culture. Instead, work to help promising up-and-comers with the niceties of business mores and protocol, so they can remain with your organization and lead it effectively.

CHAPTER 3

Give the Next Generation Room to Grow

Toward the end of the last economic expansion, the world of corporate human resources managers was abuzz over a trend called *boomeranging*. The term referred to the increasing practice of companies hiring back former employees who had left go to work for other firms, many of them Internet start-ups that seemed to offer vast wealth overnight. When the dot-coms collapsed (in almost all cases without delivering the promised riches), many of these newly unemployed former corporate brains showed up on their old employers's doorsteps looking for work. What made the trend newsworthy was not that the ex-employees wanted to return to their former places of employment; it was that the companies were willing to hire them back.

Think about that for a minute. Here we were in the middle of a generational low in unemployment, with talented workers as scarce as icicles in Death Valley. Yet everyone felt it remarkable that companies would be willing to hire back workers who had already proven themselves, were familiar with the company's policies and practices, and had left of their own free will, often after refusing lucrative offers to stay.

What does that say about the way companies nurture their next generation of leaders? What it says is that they don't do a very good job. The proof is in reports that many companies even had to bend rehiring policies—often unwritten but no less firm. Many found the newly returned workers were among their best hires, often performing better than they had on the first go-round. Like children back home after their first stab at independence, these returnees served to convince other employees, who were thinking about grazing the greener pastures, to stick with it. The boomerangs also found that they were more appreciative of what they had. In many cases, the skills they had acquired during their time away, sometimes several years, made them far more valuable to their employers.

Trying to keep employees from working elsewhere is just one way companies limit the growth of employees and damage their chance of harvesting top-shelf future leaders. They also fail to take advantage of having future leaders work closely with customers and suppliers, which could provide a good opportunity to cement relationships, open channels of communication, crossfertilize new ideas into the corporate culture, and benefit the company in many other ways.

Perhaps worst of all, many firms don't allow future leadership candidates to gain from making mistakes. Rather than place employees into positions of responsibility and accountability, where they can learn truly long-lasting lessons about business, they are frequently assigned soft bivouacs where nothing is at risk and, therefore, little is learned. Only with responsibility and accountability, with no immunity, will long-lasting lessons about business occur.

For clarity, I am only talking about rehiring an employee who leaves the company on good terms. Quitting on short notice, going to work for a direct competitor where trade secrets are at risk, or misconduct of any type qualifies as leaving on bad terms. Certainly, any employee who commits acts that are underhanded, unethical, or inappropriate should not be brought back to work under any circumstance.

Negative rehiring is a telltale sign of weak leadership. I learned this the hard way. In one of my early management positions, a manager working under me convinced me that rehiring a former employee, who had just been released from prison, was a good solution to his immediate problem and the company would be better off. He explained that prior to this man's imprisonment, he had been a productive member of his telemarketing team. The manager reasoned that everybody deserves a second chance, the man knew the company policies, and, perhaps more important, he was in a bind at that moment. I didn't like the idea but acquiesced to the rehire.

Although this individual filled a momentary opening, he created numerous and severe problems. How do I spell M-I-S-T-A-K-E? Many of the employees, especially the ladies, who worked alongside the rehire, were disgusted to discover they were working next to a parolee on a work-release program. Because of his particular gender-related offense, many actually refused to work as long as he was employed. Although this situation was clearly extreme, the real damage was that a large number of employees lost confidence in their local manager. This story was, unfortunately, shared among employees for many years, usually in a context of disrespect for this particular individual. Although I was not overly concerned about the rehire mistake, this well-intentioned manager unfortunately was never able to rebound from a reputation of being shortsighted.

OUT OF FOCUS

Carr Tilton

A businessman I'll call Carr Tilton was your stereotypical, larger-than-life Texas oilman and cattle rancher. He was raised during World War II in the hardscrabble hills of the West Texas as the oldest son in a family of cedar-choppers. He eked out a living cutting juniper trees and refining the aromatic oils in backyard cookers. His skills as a baseball player earned enough attention to warrant a college scholarship. Rejecting an offer to play minor-league baseball, he instead joined the Marines, where he distinguished himself during the Korean War's brutal Inchon amphibious landing.

Returning a decorated war hero, Tilton decided oil and real estate were the businesses to be in. Taking on the already entrenched interests of the oil industry, he won a reputation for being an exceptionally capable, self-taught geologist, driller, marketer, and financier. Over the course of three decades, Tilton built Whitetail, Inc., into a prosperous and well-respected conglomerate.

Tilton was distinguished by average intelligence but off-the-charts drive, determination, and self-assurance. The traits served him well in his rough-and-tumble endeavors. But in the context of his family, especially the son who was designated to inherit Whitetail, they were less successful.

Countless corporate anecdotes tell how Tilton put down his son, Terry, denigrating his ability and relegating him to do-nothing jobs. Perhaps the pivotal event occurred when Terry was 30 and suddenly informed his father that he planned to work elsewhere than Whitetail. To the elder Tilton, the comment was nonsensical. Other than a gruff brush-off, he ignored it. His primary response was to offer to pay Terry more than the other company was offering, and he strongly insinuated that severe penalties we be inflicted if Terry didn't take his money.

Terry, unfortunately, acquiesced to Carr's hot combination of carrot and stick. He settled into a comfortable office that was adjacent to his father's but might be on the other side of the world for all the involvement he took in the company's operation.

Now Terry is 53, has never worked anywhere else or done anything outside the shadow of his father, who never really allowed him to do so. Carr wants to retire and hand the business over to Terry. But the older man is just now realizing that running it will be impossible for his son. Is it too late for this to turn into a Portrait of Success rather than an example of why we need to give the next generation room to grow? Time will tell.

In Dallas, whenever the first freeze of winter is forecast on the evening news, doors flap citywide as people rush outside to retrieve potted plants, too delicate to survive icy temperatures, and bring them inside where they'll be snug and warm. Needless to say, the native live oak and pecan trees, the Texas sagebrush bushes, and hardy imports such as flowering crepe myrtles are left to their fate, and they do fine.

The point of this horticultural anecdote is this: you don't want your company run by a bunch of fair-weather potted plants. Future leaders must be exposed to the elements. They must acquire and demonstrate the ability to withstand the tough commercial climates in which they will operate. To develop the necessary tough skin, they need room to grow and err, and that space has to be unsheltered.

What that means in a business sense is that they must have the freedom to make decisions and be held accountable for the quality of those decisions. Only then can the saplings you have on hand today possess a good chance of growing into the type of sturdy, hardy, resistant leaders you will need to grow and build long-term, sustainable profitability and wealth.

ACTION ITEM 1

Give high-potential future leaders responsibility, accountability, and room to grow.

The General Electric Co. is arguably one of the greatest companies in the history of business, or at least the last century. It's the only original member of the Dow Jones index still in existence. GE is first or second in a broad range of global industry sectors, producing jet aircraft engines, kitchen appliances, lighting, generators, nuclear reactors, locomotives, medical imaging technology, and plastics. Its services include one of the biggest financing units in the country in GE Capital and the NBC television network. A company like that has every right to be haughty, to protect its secrets fiercely, and to adopt a stringent "not invented here" attitude.

In fact, however, GE has been one of the most outward-looking companies in existence. One of its basic stratagems is the use of strategic alliances in which it collaborates, trades information, and shares employees with other companies. In 1999, it was involved in more than 100 such alliances. One of them, with French jet engine maker Snecma, has survived almost two decades, and together these companies have manufactured jet engines worth $40 billion.

You don't have to be Jack Welch to embrace collaboration and sharing employees with other companies. Your company doesn't have to be GE to gain the benefits employees reap from working in other corporate cultures, acquiring different skills, and making contacts that can lead to the same sort of alliances that have benefitted GE so remarkably. You can get the biggest bang for your buck by exposing future leaders to other companies.

When a customer wants you to send an executive for a conference about requirements, consider delegating the task to a future leader. If a supplier asks for someone to help develop an improved ordering system, it's an opportunity to gain insight into that supplier while you train the vanguard of the next generation.

ACTION ITEM 2

Collaborate and share employees with other companies.

Specialize, specialize, specialize. In many areas of human endeavor, those words are the mantra that advisors use to help high achievers maximize their potential. Thus, we get swimmers who specialize in the 200-meter backstroke and software developers who write code only for electronically controlled automatic transmissions in cars. Without question, specialization can lead to outstanding achievement in narrow areas. But too much specialization is not appropriate for a future leader. The risk of overspecialization is that leaders will know more and more about less and less. Even if you don't, as the old joke says, "wind up knowing everything about nothing," that much specialization does not help someone guide a business through the multiplicity of ever changing challenges that, over time, bombard all commercial enterprises.

As a college student, to pay my educational and living expenses, I worked as a karate instructor at Trias International Judo and Karate. My sensei and mentor was Master Robert A. Trias. Trias was a great man, widely recognized as the father of karate in America and head of the then largest and most prestigious martial arts association in the world, the United States Karate Association. This relationship opened many doors for me in the world of martial arts, but it was not enough to break through some of the long-standing barriers to non-members of a particular school or association to compete in tournaments. I was unwelcome in many of these tournaments, which I found limiting.

However, one of my fellow instructors at Trias International was the legendary World Champion Bill "Superfoot" Wallace. Bill was known for his amazing left leg kicking techniques—undoubtedly the most advanced of any martial arts practitioner before or since. He could win almost any competition anywhere in the world using only his left leg as an offensive weapon. But what so impressed all who knew him was his unending thirst to train and spar with anybody. If a young novice was sitting quietly on the side, Bill was likely to convince them to train with him. He would go through this routine, often for six or seven hours, until he had simply exhausted the entire dojo of training partners. He was constantly entering tournaments and appearing at dojos across the world with his gi in hand, ready to train until the lights were turned off. This broad exposure coming up through the ranks had prepared him to become the undisputed world middleweight champion, with 23 title defenses, and retire undefeated.

Bill Wallace trained with as many different people as possible. He learned from anyone who could teach him. His willingness to vary from his infamous technique was, according to Bill, one of the most important things that led to his success—not only as a legendary competitor but as an internationally sought after teacher.

Karate isn't the only field in which exposure to many different methods and approaches is beneficial. In music, composers and conductors must have proficiency in a number of instruments to arrange and perform music. The same is true in business. When employees specialize, they tend to get very good at one thing. The leadership challenge is to bring together multiple specialists and, knowing each individual's potential contribution, unite them as a high performing team.

The way to avoid overspecialization in business is to give future leaders intensive exposure to many aspects of the company. Ideally, that exposure will encompass an array of functions, from operations and finance to marketing and administration. It will also include experience at a variety of levels, from entry-level salesperson to department head and, ultimately, the CEO's office.

What do you gain by this? Insight is the key benefit. When you have worked alongside people outside the executive suite, you know what their issues are, what they are thinking, what will fly and won't fly with them. When you have confronted the challenges of a number of different departments, you gain invaluable understanding of what they need, what they don't need, and what they can't tolerate.

ACTION ITEM 3

Give promising people a variety of experiences.

PORTRAIT OF SUCCESS

Robert Dedman, Jr.

Robert H. Dedman, Jr., is a member of the club. In fact, Dedman *is* the club. As CEO of privately held, Dallas-based ClubCorp, Inc., which owns and operates more than 200 golf courses, resorts, sports clubs, country clubs, business clubs, and various real estate developments around the world, Dedman is arguably the most influential person in the global club industry.

How did he get there? The main reason is that his father, Robert H. Dedman, Sr., started ClubCorp in 1957—the year Robert Jr. was born—by buying 400 acres of Dallas land and building Brookhaven Country Club.

How does he stay there? That's a good question when you consider that Dedman Sr., still the chairman of the company, is such a dynamic, high-profile executive that he was once labeled "the Henry Ford of the club management business." Following in his footsteps is not an easy task, yet Dedman Jr. is pulling it off with considerable aplomb. In fact, he's even surpassed his father in some respects, such as when he presided over the biggest deal in the history of golf with the acquisition of 24 courses from Cobblestone Golf Group.

With 23,000 employees and over $1 billion in revenues, no doubt a sinecure could have been found for Dedman Jr. somewhere in the corporation. But one of the keys to his success is that, rather than remain nestled in the protective bosom of his family company, Dedman Jr. went in search of additional experience outside ClubCorp.

To start with, he obtained an extensive educational background, earning a bachelor's degree in economics, an MBA, and a law degree. Following business school, he worked for four years at ClubCorp as director of corporate planning. Then he left ClubCorp and went to the Wall Street firm Salomon Brothers, Inc., where he specialized in mergers and acquisitions.

As director of corporate planning, Dedman Jr. helped ClubCorp respond to the fitness boom by leading it into the purchase and management of fitness clubs, sports clubs, and related facilities. In 1987, after his stint at Salomon, he returned to ClubCorp as chief financial officer. He became president and chief operating officer in January 1989. Nine years later, he was named chief executive officer.

His varied experiences haven't diluted his loyalty to the company one iota. According to his father, "Bob has ClubCorp in his blood."

Computer software can do some amazing things. From tasks such as calculating a spreadsheet to graphically displaying an exciting action game, software's abilities far outstrip the capacities of its human creators. But humans still remain paramount in one area, and that is the ability to learn from our mistakes. If you've ever entered the wrong formula in a spreadsheet cell or typed an incorrect address into a Web browser, you know that the software will, without fail, produce incorrect results. With a few rare exceptions among artificial intelligence implementations, software doesn't learn from mistakes—not yet.

People not only learn when they make mistakes, but sometimes they get the best learning experience from making the biggest mistakes. If you write off a person from the leadership track because of an error, especially a truly egregious one, then you may just have written off one of the most qualified candidates for the future.

In the early 1990s, the photography industry experienced a surge of interest in something called glamour photography. These specialty portraits involved lengthy sessions of two, even three hours. A professional cosmetologist would poof the hair, apply glamorizing make-up, and assist in the selection of the most flattering fashions for a "cover girl" photo session. The object was to create an exhilarating, "new you" customer experience and preserve it on film.

Glamour photography was a highly specialized endeavor, and customers loved the end result. Following a competitor, Olan Mills, Inc., jumped into this new market. Although the idea to do so was not mine, I confess that I quickly became seduced by the flashy upscale fashion mall surroundings, customer enthusiasm, and the resulting incredible sales averages.

What I clearly knew, but chose to ignore, was that glamour photography required a completely different business model—one that was unfamiliar to me at the time. Instead of strip-center space renting for $10 a square foot, we committed to mall leases at three to five times that amount. Construction time surged from less than 2 weeks to, in some cases, over 90 days, with construction costs geometrically higher. We had to purchase and provide cosmetic products, admittedly something I still know next to nothing about. Staffing hours were sky high. Instead of a standard 40-hour a week studio, mall locations required staffing 72 hours each week, including Sundays and almost every holiday.

Marketing glamour was significantly different from the tried-and-true telemarketing methods I knew like the back of my hand.

This new venture depended upon walk-in traffic, word-of-mouth referrals, and name recognition—marketing approaches generally unfamiliar to me at that time. All fads eventually meet their doom. When the glamour fad faded, we were saddled with heavy, upfront construction costs and commitments for long-term leases, not to mention enough make-up to paint all of the actresses in Hollywood through the next decade.

The point of telling this story is to highlight it as a learning experience. This short-lived venture taught me many lessons that I have carried into other settings. For example, I understand better the concepts and importance of value-drivers, core competencies, competitive advantage, pilot programs, outside perspectives, and not letting enthusiasm for new projects get in the way of good judgement.

I dare say every seasoned CEO has lived through similar experiences. Nobody at the top can claim "no mistakes" in their past, and if they try, watch out. Expensive? Yes, but there is no vicarious substitution. Learning from mistakes is important—required—for long-term leadership success.

Back to martial arts for a moment. Bodhidharma, a Buddhist monk from India, is credited with developing what would later become known broadly as the martial arts. Around 520 A.D., Bodhidharma attempted to walk from India, over the Himalayas, into China. The physical challenge of the high altitudes and harsh conditions of such a journey forced him to retreat to his homeland seven times. Determined to succeed by overcoming the harsh environment, he began mimicking the graceful and tight motions of the native animals such as the mantis, the tiger, and the leopard, and he patterned exercises after their conservative movements. Combining his newly acquired physical strength with his deepening spirituality, Bodhidharma successfully crossed over on his eighth attempt. Thus the expression, "Seven times failure, eighth time success."

Bodhidharma could have given in to the elements of nature, but he didn't. Failure, it seems, only fueled his determination to succeed. Once in China, he passed down the spiritual and physical lessons that brought him success. His willingness to take enormous risk, and to experience failure, eventually formed the foundations of kung fu, tai chi, and karate.

ACTION ITEM 4:

Encourage future leaders to take appropriate risks, and let them make mistakes.

In *The Oxford Dictionary of Quotations,* you can find nearly 100 different quotable comments on forgiving and forgetting. They range from Jesus—"Father, forgive them, for they know not what they do."—to Oscar Wilde—"Children begin by loving their parents; after a while they judge them; rarely, if ever, do they forgive them." Forgiveness is clearly considered an important topic in the world in general.

What about the business world? When I searched an online database of more than 15,000 quotations, I found precisely zero including the words *forgive* and *business.* Quotes having to do with *forgetting* tended to be like the one attributed to cosmetics executive Elizabeth Arden, who told her husband, "Dear, never forget one little point: It's my business. You just work here." Ahem.

Yet the power of forgiveness is an overlooked asset in business. That's especially true when it comes to nurturing future leaders. If you are unwilling to forgive someone for an error in judgment, then you are probably setting an unreasonably high bar for selecting future leaders.

Many leaders are shortsighted and feel the need for draconian steps when mistakes occur. Of course, some offenses require summary dismissal—violations of law or ethics, or breaches of confidentiality or trust, for example. But if somebody has made a judgment that turns out wrong, you have to ride with it. Don't give a promising future leader responsibility and then fire them the first time they screw up. An atmosphere where mistakes are considered learning opportunities and are a contribution to longer-term success will foster open communication, and it will move the organization toward becoming a "learning organization." Let people make some minor mistakes.

Think about Thomas Edison and the thousands of failures that he experienced developing the incandescent light bulb. Would you have fired Edison when he failed after the first stab? Hopefully not.

ACTION ITEM 5

Be willing to forgive and forget.

OUT OF FOCUS

Katz's Deli

Marc Katz Is the son of a New York deli owner and the grandson and great-grandson of kosher butchers. As the owner of Katz's Deli and Bar in Austin, he is also the undisputed dean of delicatessen owners in the Texas capital. Since 1979, Katz's has been a landmark on Sixth Street in the city, and his catchphrase has become part of the city's lexicon, thanks to the television commercials that invariably end with the grinning founder uttering, "I can't help it. I gotta tell ya—Katz's Never Closes."

Now it looks like Katz's may close forever, and the cause is— I can't help it, I gotta tell ya—an inability between the founder and his son to agree that, though mistakes have been made, they need to forgive, forget, and forge on. The problem, as laid out in a lawsuit the elder Katz filed asking a judge to order the eatery sold, is that Barry Katz drained money from the Austin establishment in order to back an expansion location in Houston. The two own the original location together, with the semiretired father retaining 51 percent, while the son owns the Houston location.

Specifically, Marc says Barry used the original deli's credit to borrow $1 million, which he then lent interest-free to the second restaurant, 2020. Katz the elder also complains that Barry's restaurant was improperly compensating the Austin location for handling its administrative tasks. Finally, his dad deemed Barry's $414,000 annual salary from the Austin restaurant excessive.

Barry said the charges were untrue or misrepresentations and that he and his father had agreed on the decisions together. Meanwhile, the conflict was destined for court, and Katz's 20-year-plus run in Austin appeared near its end, at least as a Katz family venture. "I've turned it over to the courts," Marc said.

Without going so far as to say who may be wrong, a "leave it to the court" attitude won't keep the business going. A more forgiving and promising note was sounded by 30-year-old Barry, who said, "Partners have and resolve disputes, and we'll resolve this matter."

Many of the things you have to do to develop leaders capable of generating long-term success are counterintuitive. It doesn't seem sensible that you can create loyalty by encouraging a valued employee to work somewhere else. But that's how it works. Incestuous development is a greater risk in family businesses. A client in the food service industry was commanded to join the family business with no thought as to whether he wanted to or, better, was able to perform. The lack of outside experience and, frankly, motivation eventually doomed the company. Rather than obligating family members to join, give them room to decide if coming on board is right for them. If they do join, have a family employment policy that rewards working and achieving elsewhere. It goes against the grain to consider allying with another company when your own people are probably capable of doing the job on their own. But alliances really are a good idea. You would think that for a leader to perform at a high level, she would have to specialize in one or more areas and become exceedingly expert. But a generalist is actually likely to perform better. As for people who make mistakes—can they really benefit from realizing that they've screwed up? Yes, they can.

Finally, forgiving and forgetting sometimes feel like the most expensive and painful tools for managing that have ever been conceived. But, actually, they cost us nothing. By giving the next generation of leaders the space they need to grow, without fear that any misstep will doom them forever, forgiving and forgetting can be among the most powerful methods for growing excellent managers you will ever use.

ACTION ITEMS

ACTION ITEM 1
Give high-potential future leaders responsibility, accountability, and room to grow.

ACTION ITEM 2
Collaborate and share employees with other companies.

ACTION ITEM 3
Give promising people a variety of experiences.

ACTION ITEM 4
Encourage future leaders to take appropriate risks and let them make mistakes.

ACTION ITEM 5
Be willing to forgive and forget.

CHAPTER 4

Finding a Common Direction

At about the time Olan Mills, Inc., was taking its first steps on the path to becoming the world's largest portrait photography firm, two events occurred, by chance, that decades later would create serious difficulties for the company's studios and virtually threaten their existence.

In 1935, the world's first automatic telephone answering machine was invented. It was favored by Orthodox Jews whose religious practices prohibited answering the telephone on the Sabbath. This new technology device, however, was too bulky and costly to become widely popular. Not until the 1960s were compact, affordable, easy-to-use answering machines introduced in the United States. Over the course of the next three decades, they would be refined into low-cost, simple, digital devices that were all but ubiquitous in American homes.

The 1930s also saw the rise in power of Adolph Hitler and the German Nazi Party, which would lead to World War II and the mobilization of the Allies's economic resources to a degree never seen before or since. That mobilization included the entry of millions of women into the workforce, a change that today accounts for women making up nearly one half the adult labor pool in America.

The combination of women being away from home, working in factories and offices, while answering machines took calls on the home phone essentially jerked the rug out from under telemarketers. Olan Mills, Inc.'s, marketing practices had long rested on targeting mothers, contacted at home during the day, and selling them a Club Plan, our version of a continuity program. Once purchased, the Club Plan brought customers into an Olan Mills studio several times each year. It was all but impossible to sell portrait photography plans to answering machines and, increasingly, that's what Olan Mills, Inc., and other business-to-consumer telemarketers encountered when dialing into homes.

You can't expect to be in business without encountering occasional major disruptions in the way you generate income. Surely, almost every business that succeeds over a period of many years has to face one or more similar instances. But this particular circumstance proved to be a watershed event in Olan Mills, Inc.'s, history.

The problem was that some thought the members of the sales force had become lazy and were not as dedicated as the old timers who had performed so well in the past. Others knew that the climate had changed and old expectations of telemarketing performance were now unrealistic. Yet another faction thought the debate irrelevant, as social pressure would soon force new legislation that would outlaw telemarketing. (This never occurred, although many states did regulate telemarketing practices.) Massive disagreement ensued on how to deal with this shift, and employees chose sides, eventually causing an impasse and delaying meaningful changes in the company's marketing approach. As telemarketing steadily became less effective under the relentless influence of major trends, the number of new customers fell, and market share eroded.

While accurately predicting major social, technological, and legal changes is not always possible, anybody who was involved with the company at that time could easily forecast trouble. The seeds of the company's newest struggle were sown, not just by answering machines and women employed outside the home, but by open disagreement on the company's marketing strategies. A refrain echoed throughout many companies: "We have a problem and can't agree on how to fix it, so do nothing."

Louis V. Gerstner, Jr., the celebrated executive who restored International Business Machines Corp. to health after the computer giant stumbled, was asked in 1993 when he took the top job at Big Blue whether he planned to create a new vision for the suffering company. "The last thing we need around here is vision," Gerstner replied. But, as events proved, Gerstner did have a very clear vision for what IBM should do. It just wasn't lofty enough to conform to what most people's idea of vision was at the time. Instead of spouting airy maxims, Gerstner crafted strategies for each of IBM's important businesses and then soberly executed them. IBM bloomed, and Gerstner gave a new meaning and importance to the concept of business vision.

Long-term business success is impossible unless leaders share a common vision and common goals on everything from marketing methods to the business's basic purpose. I call it *finding a common direction.*

This book focuses on creating long-term business success. I can guarantee you this: your company will, over time, face at least one upheaval very similar to those I experienced at Olan Mills, Inc. Thousands of very capable companies both large and small, public and private, face business threats each quarter. When those life-threatening challenges arise, the extent to which leadership can find a common direction and get key people to rally around it may well be the ultimate factor determining if the company will overcome the hurdles and realize long-term prosperity, or fade away into obscurity.

LACK OF COMMON DIRECTION: A MAJOR RISK

Testing is an important part of business strategy. You test-market to see what products, advertisements, and messages work best. You test technologies to see which can do the job. You test people, either by trying them out in various jobs or by administering tests and evaluations, to determine whether their skills and abilities are adequate and matched to specific tasks. But there is a time and place for testing. Businesses that go overboard and want to test every single thing, even concrete decisions that have already been decided, may be unable to act decisively and quickly. Business is not like cooking pasta, where you toss strands of pasta against the wall to see if they stick. Not everything in a business is or should be open for debate. It's important for leaders to lead, not simply conduct popularity polls to find out which direction looks best to the most people.

When the people in a company do not agree about the direction and strategy of the organization, the company becomes like a ship at sea with no rudder or destination. Or, worse, like a ship that has people struggling over the rudder, steering first one way and then another, as the various combatants manage temporarily to assert their wills. Such companies risk winding up like a host of Internet companies, who at the turn of the millennium raised many millions for business models that had no chance of generating significant revenues, much less profits.

In some of these enterprises, investors watched their cash burn away on hopeless strategies as a company spasmodically lurched from one new idea to another. Managers would abandon the original plans and a series of subsequent plans so quickly that, even if one of them had been viable, management was out the door and onto a new concept before anything could take shape.

Netpliance, an Austin, Texas, company now known as Tipping-Point Technologies, Inc., is a good example. Netpliance started out with a widely reported—and very well capitalized—plan to sell a so-called Internet appliance called the *i-opener*. The i-opener was supposed to provide very low-cost access to e-mail and the World Wide Web. But the idea never took off. Sales peaked at just under $4 million in Netpliance's best quarter, ending in September of 2000, and its net loss was more than ten times that. At that rate, Netpliance would burn through its remaining $12 million cash reserve in no time.

The company licensed its technology to others and was able to raise more money, but in the meantime, the Internet appliance idea had lost its luster. In 2001, Netpliance sold off its subscriber base, changed its name to TippingPoint Technologies, and got completely out of the hardware business. The new plan was to do something totally different: offer services for high-speed Internet access. That's a pretty big turnaround for a company only a few years old. At last report, TippingPoint had essentially no sales but around $60 million in the bank. Its market value, meanwhile, was less than half of what it had been when it was in the Internet appliance business.

The risk generated by a lack of a consistent, common direction is obvious. But not all of the dangers associated with failing to achieve consensus are so plain. One of the most insidious hazards is choosing the least objectionable strategy or the path of least resistance. In this scenario, two or more people, who are ostensibly focused on leading the company, are actually in the business of quietly battling each other for control. To avoid open confrontation, they jointly choose not the best strategy, but one to which nobody strongly objects. The company takes a route that is not necessarily intended to maximize longevity and success but to minimize internal conflict. This approach frequently results in more conflict, not less, and any long-term, sustainable success that results is accidental and unlikely.

Perhaps more common is a leader doing nothing when faced with dissenters to the strategy he would like to pursue. The leader is either unable or unwilling to take on the job of convincing others to follow. In any event, the leader simply abdicates leadership. In rare cases, no decisions are made, no changes take place, and the company simply drifts along in the same general direction. In an even moderately changing business environment, this is clearly no recipe for regeneration and success. In this scenario, abdicating leadership to avoid conflict is a prescription for stagnation and eventual decline. Another scenario is more likely and, in some ways, more unsettling. In the absence of clear leadership and direction, people other than the titular leader ultimately will decide a direction for the company. Whether this will be a beneficial direction depends on how well they make this selection and their ulterior motives. Leaders must provide direction, or others will.

ACTION ITEM 1

Effective leaders articulate a compelling and understandable common direction.

PORTRAIT OF SUCCESS

George Steinbrenner

Long-time New York Yankees owner George Steinbrenner is probably at the top of the list of people whom other people love to hate. Almost nothing about Steinbrenner is particularly endearing. He has a penchant for firing people in a particularly insensitive fashion, publicly dumping legendary manager Billy Martin five times and hiring him back four times. He has almost no respect for his so-called superiors either. Major League Baseball ordered him to surrender control of the Yankees because of his dealings with a small-time gambler, and since his reinstatement in 1993, he has been anything but apologetic.

George Michael Steinbrenner III was born on July 4, 1930, in Rocky River, Ohio, and was a successful athlete in high school and at Williams College. After graduating from Williams, a small liberal arts college in the Northeast, he served in the Air Force before joining the family firm, American Shipbuilding of Cleveland. He eventually became president of that firm, but only entered the public eye in 1973 when he purchased the Yankee franchise from then owner CBS.

During the next few decades, Steinbrenner revealed himself as an exceedingly short-tempered, contradictory, and even impulsive business leader. For example, he changed managers 21 times in his first 27 years at the helm. Paradoxically, he was also sometimes slow to learn. After his unparalleled hiring of costly free agent talents led to the Yankees's first World Series championship in 1979, the Boss, as he is known, stuck with the free-agent strategy and ignored the development of players through the minor league system. Combined with his frequent firings of star players who disputed his authority, the result was more than a decade of mediocrity.

But Steinbrenner retained his relentless focus on winning, and during the 1980s showed he had learned his lesson by redeveloping the Yankees's farm system. Beginning in 1996, with its bench stocked with a potent blend of home-grown and free-agent stars, the Yankees went on a tear, winning the first of what would be four World Series titles in the last five years of the millennium, including three straight before the Arizona Diamondbacks upset their run in 2001.

The total number of Yankees Series championships through 2001 was 26, making the "Bronx Bombers" the most successful franchise in professional sports. Not coincidentally, they are also the most valuable team, worth an estimated three-quarters of a billion dollars. Compare that to the miserly $14 million

Steinbrenner paid CBS for the team in 1973. There's no doubt that, love him or hate him, the Boss's mix of passion, vision, irascibility, and success makes him the greatest owner of the greatest team in sports history—the benefit of all stakeholders having the same common direction.

If you grow up in Texas and live 7.2 miles from the stadium where the NFL's Dallas Cowboys pulled off many of their history-making victories, football is like barbecue: you cannot go far before you miss it. So I hope you'll excuse a football metaphor that is particularly appropriate to this topic. America's legendary team coached by Tom Landry had one common goal: to reach and win the Super Bowl, the pinnacle of professional football achievement. For a given player on any given play, the individual goal might to be gain yardage or to prevent a tackler from reaching the Cowboys quarterback. But the common goal for everyone was to win the championship, something they accomplished more than almost any other football club. Individual goals, motives, and viewpoints had to be subordinate to this overarching plan.

Sam Walton, founder of the world's largest retailer, once said that Wal-Mart's purpose was to "provide ordinary folks with the goods and services normally purchased by rich people." That is crystal clear vision, the kind that everybody can relate to and support. At Wal-Mart it worked. In the same way, every company does best when every employee (ideally every stakeholder) is on the same page. At the very least, top executives should be working off the same plan and should agree on strategy. If they cannot agree on strategy, they can at least agree to suppress their disagreement for the common good. The benefits of having a common direction are many, some comprehensive in their advantages, others more subtle. By any measure, one of the most vital benefits of getting everyone to execute the same plan is that business leaders are relieved of having to micromanage everything.

Think of it. When you are trying to execute a plan that does not have the full support of the people who are supposed to be executing it, your job is tripled. You have to personally see that every single detail of the process is carried out. You may even have to insist on things being done over and over until the unwilling participants are bullied (or wearied) into doing them right. When everyone is in agreement on the strategy, the leader's job is a piece of cake. You do not have to closely supervise execution. You can give subordinates the plan or the goal and let them run with it, knowing that they will execute according to the master strategy upon which you have agreed. This can free up massive amounts of management time, which is one of the scarcest resources at almost every closely held business.

Getting agreement on an organization's direction does more than relieve management of minutiae. When everyone knows and agrees on the overall direction of the company, everyone becomes a manager with an eye on the prize. Lower-level managers assign tasks and coordinate projects in such a way as to maximize their effect on the agreed-upon objectives. That holds true all the way down to the lowest level employees. When a counter service clerk is faced with a demanding customer insisting upon a refund, the clerk can handle the problem without resorting to a policy manual or seeking their supervisor's blessing. But this happens only if the company's overall direction is clear and communicated to all levels in the organization. The leveraging effect is hard to overstate.

ACTION ITEM 2

Use your common direction to present a consistent image to employees, customers, and prospects.

Don't think that the benefits of having a common direction are limited to management, either. When everyone in an organization knows just where that organization is going, they will present a consistent image to all customers and prospects. This is more than a simplistic "the customer is always right" dogma. The customer isn't always right, of course.

But for some companies, it doesn't really matter. For instance, because Olan Mills was the most recognizable name in the portrait industry, both my grandfather and uncle felt a responsibility to the entire industry. Their reasoning: If the industry grows, Olan Mills will continue to gain market share. People who have a bad experience with another studio might walk away and never set foot in an Olan Mills studio. To combat this possible negative outcome, they established a very high standard for dealing with unhappy customers. Olan Mills would replace, at no charge, any product that the customer was unhappy with—for any reason.

As a "wet behind the ears" employee learning the ropes in Phoenix, Arizona, I was confronted by an elder man in our Christown Shopping Mall studio. He had a very old photo album that he had purchased from a door-to-door salesman 25 years earlier, while he was still living in Maine. His complaint: When he had purchased the photo plan, he was supposed to have received two photo shoots and two 8"×10" color photos each year for 20 years. He had missed the last 13 years of the plan. Now the plan had expired, and he just wanted his money back.

Dismissing the old man would have been easy because it was absolutely clear that Olan Mills had nothing to do with his album contract. All Olan Mills photos carry a distinctive logo, which his photos were missing. Further, at the time he purchased his plan, we had no stores in the entire state of Maine. None of this mattered, however, as this man only knew one name in the industry—Olan Mills—and he was standing in front of me causing a fuss. I called my boss and explained the unusual story. Without hesitation, I was instructed to write a refund request and offer him a complimentary photo session.

Every organization has limits to what it will do for customers. That's neither good nor bad, but what is unquestionably bad is when a customer gets one story from one person and a different story from someone else. You can't necessarily ensure consistency just by making sure your customer service policies are clearly spelled out, either. As everyone who has customers knows, issues arise frequently that are too new, too unusual, or too complex to be addressed by a customer service policy. When that happens, the only way to make sure customers are treated consistently is to have an overarching master corporate objective that has been clearly defined and absorbed by everyone in the company, especially the person with customer contact.

Practically speaking, make sure that everyone in your company knows what customer service policies say and why they say it, and understands how they tie into the company's overall direction. Only then can you expect customers to experience a consistent image of what you can do for them.

FINDING A COMMON DIRECTION

The General Electric Co. is the only member of the original Dow Jones index that is still an independent operating company. It has also generally, depending on stock price fluctuations, been the world's most valuable enterprise, with a stock market capitalization that has been worth one-half trillion U.S. dollars. It cemented its position as perhaps the world's most admired company during the 20-year reign of CEO Jack Welch. Welch is, of course, identified as the innovator of many important management concepts. But one of his most enduring is likely to be his insistence that the company always be either first or second in market share in the many markets in which it operates. Otherwise, in Welch's terse dictum, he would, "Fix it, sell it, or close it." Any of GE's more than a quarter-million employees could easily grasp that guide and use it to make a wide array of decisions. As common directions go, it's perhaps the gold standard.

ACTION ITEM 3

Clearly identify and express a corporate purpose that relates to shareholder concerns.

Finding a common direction always starts with identifying the purpose of the company. This may sound elementary—aren't all companies set up to make money? Actually, however, purposes vary widely among the organizations I have worked with. Some companies are set up to build market share quickly and then, according to plan, sell out to public investors or other companies interested in entering the field. Many startups had this objective during the Internet and technology frenzy of the late 1990s, for instance. At the other end of the spectrum, other companies may be set up with very little intention of pursuing growth. These may be little more than private employment agencies for family and friends of a closely held enterprise.

One common mistake among business leaders is to focus overly on the competition. To be sure, every company faces or will face significant competition. But leadership, in large part, is setting a direction for long-term success based on what that particular organization wants to become. What other companies are, or want to be, must be secondary to that concern. Being driven solely by a desire to beat the competition rather than, say, maximize talents will lead you to play catch-up rather than to set the pace yourself. By all means, include data about the competition in deliberations, but don't become obsessed.

Your objective does have one ironclad requirement. It must relate to the concerns of the shareholders, whether they are members of the public, members of a family, or members of a small but unrelated group of owners. Other than that, legitimate company purposes may include anything from maximizing quarterly net profits to providing tax losses for the owners to offset gains from other investments. Some companies even include among their objectives a desire to effect social change. Companies such as The Body Shop and Ben & Jerry's Ice Cream are well-known examples of environmentally supportive or "green" organizations. Whatever your objective, you have to know it before you can even begin to set a common direction.

ACTION ITEM 4

The methods you employ to lead your business must have an ethical foundation and match up with the corporate objectives you are pursuing.

Methods are the next thing to consider, and it's important to begin at ground level. That is, ask yourself: What are acceptable methods to achieve common direction objectives? All corporate decisions are made within an ethical framework. These days, those ethical frameworks can be complex. You may have to make decisions about whether you are going to employ technology that may infringe on another company's patent, for example. You may have to decide whether you will use certain information you have collected about your customers in your future marketing campaigns, or whether you will consider that information private and not to be exploited. New laws may change strategies in a single penstroke.

Practically speaking, the methods you employ have to fit those corporate objectives. For instance, if your enterprise has committed itself to rapid growth, that goal is not consistent with entering slow-growth markets with trailing-edge technology products and little investment in marketing. At its most detailed level, matching corporate objectives with corporate direction is a spreadsheet exercise, in which projected returns from business initiatives must match stated goals. But long before you get down to the individual cells in next year's forecast, you must have common objectives and a big-picture plan for achieving them.

The time frame is a vital determinant of the methods to employ. A plan that will take five years before fruition must employ greatly different methods and resources than one that is supposed to kick out benefits in the next quarter. *Portraits of Success* is a book about long-term sustainable success, so I am biased toward time frames measured in decades instead of quarters. But even a long-range strategy must incorporate short-range objectives. You have to fit your methods to your time frame, so get straight on the time frame before proceeding to choose the means.

Provide Information

Your corporate direction may be obvious to you, but you make a serious mistake if you assume that other people will naturally or easily figure it out. Achieving a common direction requires a great deal of emphasis on communication, and that includes two-way communication as well as edicts handed down from corporate executives.

ACTION ITEM 5

Make sure you communicate your chosen corporate direction comprehensively and credibly to all employees throughout your organization.

The most important characteristic about communicating corporate direction is that it must be comprehensive in terms of the information and in its dissemination throughout the organization, and it must be credible. That doesn't mean you have to tell everybody everything, but you do have to make sure that everyone who should know, does know. And you have to make it believable.

Everybody in the organization has to understand what the company is about. This must involve more than merely explaining corporate strategy to senior executives. An effective effort to create a common direction must involve feedback. You can get feedback in many ways, from setting aside time for Q&A sessions at meetings to setting up anonymous, confidential suggestion boxes. The very best technique for gathering feedback is the time-tested "walk around." By simply walking around, and asking questions, and then truly listening to the ideas and concerns of the people throughout the organization, a leader models her interest in feedback. Even with "open door" executive policies, not everyone in the organization has equal access to the senior leadership. Meeting people on their turf facilitates an open exchange and dialogue. (Compare this with a group of employees barging into a CEOs office to give a little feedback.)

Nothing is foolproof. But you can improve the amount and quality of feedback you get by honestly asking for it and by providing a multitude of ways for employees to deliver it. To combat a lack of feedback, one client company implemented a novel approach: they based performance evaluations on how much feedback each manager obtained. When careerists understand that promotions and salary raises are contingent upon their getting information to flow upward to the executive suite, those channels will open wide.

Now, what do you tell them? It's a fact that not everyone in a company needs to know everything. Still, do not neglect financial details. Financial numbers are the vital signs of a business. Hiding them from other people in the company is like concealing the cholesterol level of a person at risk for a heart attack. Precisely what financial information you choose to share with people in your company is up to you. You may have nothing more than a chart showing yearly sales on the shop floor to let employees know how the company is meeting its financial goals.

A Dallas, Texas, engineering, architectural, and construction firm shares all information with employees at all levels—from the most seasoned vice president to the construction laborer to the receptionist. In fact, when I first asked the CEO about sharing financial information with everyone, he replied, "Yes, we share all of our financial data, each week and each quarter." For clarification, I asked, "Does that mean you share it with the receptionist next to the elevator bank?" "Yes, her too," he replied. Only later did I discover that the receptionist was also his sister and the second largest shareholder. Whether you choose to share critical information with everyone or only with those who need to know, do not expect managers or other employees to make wise decisions when they have no idea about the current status of the company, expressed in financial terms. Equally important, managers must understand the desired long-term financial position.

ACTION ITEM 6

In outlining your corporate direction, describe the company's weaknesses and challenges in addition to its strengths and opportunities. Then, clearly outline how you plan to overcome the obstacles in your path.

Now, bear in mind, when you deal with humans and not paper cutouts, legitimate questions and doubts will surface. People will not respond favorably to any direction if you ignore the obvious. So plainly express the weaknesses of your company, at least internally. Point out the uncertainties of your plan and your prospects—they certainly exist and everybody knows that. Trying to pretend that everything is fine when it's not, or that the chances of failure are nil, will only erode your credibility. That doesn't mean sounding the alarm, however. It may mean pointing out that your competition is entrenched or your margins are under pressure. Explaining how your plan will address those issues and asking for everyone's help in resolving them builds commitment. (Remember: People tend to support what they help to create.) Do not fear revealing that you have placed bets on how the future will turn out and that future bets are always uncertain. The simple fact is that people tend to respond well to candor. Use it, and your ability to create a common direction will soar.

Finding a common direction isn't always easy. Sometimes, you are able to get everyone on the same program simply by identifying and highlighting the precise differences between viewpoints. Next, get those involved to agree to disagree for the sake of the enterprise. But a common direction may bring hard choices, sometimes requiring the departure of leaders who can't join the common endeavor.

Finding a common direction doesn't mean stamping out disagreement. As Henry Ford said, "Disagreement is inevitable. If two people in an organization agree on everything, one of them is superfluous." Indeed, you'll find it impossible to avoid disagreements entirely. The question is: How do you deal with disagreement when it inevitably appears? If possible, ignore it. A certain amount of contentiousness is expected and even positive. It keeps people alert and aware of alternatives and opportunities to improve. It pushes thinking "outside the box." Contention certainly becomes a problem when it impedes organizational progress. If disagreements are causing an organization to fail to do what needs to be done, those disagreements must be brought into line and, if necessary, the persons who are disagreeing must be reassigned or released.

It may simply be time for a disgruntled employee to find a new place to work. That's especially true if they don't agree with the fundamental direction of the company or with an important operating principle. When such a situation presents itself, you may be asked to grant a variance and you may be tempted to do so. But recall—we're talking about sustained success. Over a long time, a pattern of granting exemptions to people who impede the progress and impair the health of the organization will not build wealth.

Disagreement for the sake of disagreement is also destructive. Some people seem to relate to the world in a contentious manner. Their personal policy is rarely to agree to anything. They will always find a way to disagree. The corporate world has no room for protesters. Unreasonable dissent should not be tolerated.

At Olan Mills, the basic nagging problem was that technology changed the effectiveness of telemarketing drastically. At first this change went unnoticed, although the signs were there in the form of rising costs for customer acquisition and decreasing effectiveness of telemarketing. After a while, telemarketing, which had been a profit center for the company, stopped contributing to revenue and became a cost center. Yet, despite these seemingly clear signs that a change was due, corrective action was slow to occur.

ACTION ITEM 7

Common direction is a guide, but it should not allow the company to shut off disconfirming data that suggest that even if vision and direction can be the same, strategy and tactics need to be reconsidered.

The reasons for a slow transition to alternative marketing methods deserve some comment. Telemarketing had been Olan Mills Studios's marketing standby for many years, and early on it had been a very effective marketing tool. The company had invested heavily in call centers, employees, training, and other telemarketing infrastructure. The reluctance to jettison any portion of this approach was understandable. But it was very clear that as society charged onward and answering machine usage increased, telemarketing fortunes decreased. In the absence of any sign or method for changing answering machine usage trends, telemarketing was simply going to collapse, and studio operations would be forced to find a new way to sell its services and products.

That's in hindsight, which is always unfair to those who had to make decisions without its crystalline benefit. The purpose of this story is not to indite anyone but rather to highlight the critical importance of all leadership sharing a common direction. The company did eventually leave telemarketing completely, though not before financial damage had been done. The problems we faced are similar to those most, if not all, companies will face during their pursuit of long-term wealth building. In hindsight, the firm would have done much better if all the various factions had simply agreed to a direction—any direction—and either suppressed their respective differences or had dissenters leave the company. None of these alternatives happened, and the company was the worse for it.

PORTRAIT OF SUCCESS

Dell and Compaq

Dell Computer Corporation is arguably the leading business success story of the 1990s. Michael Dell started the company in 1984, assembling computers in his University of Texas dorm room from off-the-shelf components and selling them direct to local businesses and consumers. During the last decade of the millennium, with the company still following the direct sales method, shares of Dell Computer increased in value a staggering 88,000 percent. Dell's single attempt to distribute computers via the conventional retail sales channel was a disaster, and the company never repeated the experiment. Today Dell still sells direct and only direct, and every employee from Michael Dell on down knows that.

Not far down the road from Dell, Compaq Computer Corp. was put on the computer map in Houston. Compaq's quality, innovative designs and access to leading technology made it the hands-down favorite when many corporations and consumers chose personal computers. For much of the 1990s, Compaq was the world's leading maker of personal computers. Suddenly that changed. Experts say the company, a few years older than Dell, lost its direction and began doing all sorts of things that muddied the founding vision of Rod Canion and the other former Texas Instruments executives. First, the company purchased Tandem, a maker of fault-tolerant computers used for demanding business and government applications where even brief downtime was unacceptable. Although still skirting the computing industry, this was clearly a very different field for Compaq.

Compaq probably made an even bigger mistake when it gobbled up ailing Digital Equipment Corp., a computer industry pioneer in the minicomputer field. The struggle to absorb DEC and accommodate its vastly different business needs consumed Compaq's leaders and the company's energy for years.

At Dell, meanwhile, the company never strayed from its common vision that all agreed on: to sell high quality personal computers direct to companies and individuals. Over the years, they began selling workstations and Web servers, which are arguably somewhat different from standard desktop PCs. But this change has been gradual and evolutionary. It has never, like Compaq, ventured far outside its original field in minicomputers or fault-tolerant computing. Dell's internal consistency has powered it to become the globe's leading personal computer company. At this writing, Compaq has been acquired by the Hewlett-Packard Company.

ACTION ITEMS

ACTION ITEM 1
Effective leaders articulate a compelling and understandable common direction.

ACTION ITEM 2
Use your common direction to present a consistent image to employees, customers, and prospects.

ACTION ITEM 3

Clearly identify and express a corporate purpose that relates to shareholder concerns.

ACTION ITEM 4

The methods you employ to lead your business must have an ethical foundation and match up with the corporate objectives you are pursuing.

ACTION ITEM 5

Make sure you communicate your chosen corporate direction comprehensively and credibly to all employees throughout your organization.

ACTION ITEM 6

In outlining your corporate direction, describe the company's weaknesses and challenges in addition to its strengths and opportunities. Then, clearly outline how you plan to overcome the obstacles in your path.

ACTION ITEM 7

Common direction is a guide, but it should not allow the company to shut off disconfirming data that suggest that even if vision and direction can be the same, strategy and tactics need to be reconsidered.

CHAPTER 5

Make Communication Central

I can honestly say that I have never been called in to consult with a company where the owners, managers, and employees were satisfied with their internal communication. People lament that they don't know what's going on, that their ideas fall on deaf ears. Of course, I am typically only called in when owners or senior mangers are facing serious problems of one sort or another. But communication problems are so universal that if your company encounters a crisis, the likely culprit will be a breakdown of communication.

Horrific disasters are often tied to communication failures. What else but a breakdown in communication between law enforcement and intelligence agencies allowed hijackers to plot and execute the September 11, 2001, terrorist attacks? Such breakdowns aren't new. America's worst disaster occurred 101 years and 3 days before the World Trade Center towers collapsed. More than 6,000 residents of Galveston, Texas, died when a tidal wave engulfed the city. The U.S. Weather Bureau knew a tsunami-like storm was in the Gulf of Mexico but was unable to communicate a timely warning.

Even more poignant, and more notorious, is the sinking of the Titanic. Although 1,523 men, women, and children died in that April 14, 1912, disaster, the body count would have been much higher had not the vessel's state-of-the-art wireless rig enabled operators to direct rescue vessels to the sinking ship. Moreover, fewer people would have died if nearby ships had left their wireless receivers turned on overnight. This tragedy was responsible for the Federal Radio Act of 1912, which provided for, among other things, 24-hour radio monitoring by all ships at sea. This legislation has saved countless lives since.

Why bring up the Titanic, Galveston, and the World Trade Center? While a failure to communicate in business may not result in thousands of deaths, it's still a tragedy if a company goes under because of a problem that could have been solved.

Besides being common, communication difficulties are usually at the very core of the most serious problems and missed opportunities of every company. Indeed, a failure of communication inevitably foreshadows the failure of the organization. At their most basic, businesses are groups of people who gain power and prosperity by leveraging their collective effort. Without coordination—which is achieved only by effective communication—a business is nothing but a gathering of individuals, each pursuing her own distinct agenda. This is a mob, not an organization. Never say never, but in this instance, it's true: a business lacking effective communication can *never* succeed over the long term and, very often, not even for the short run.

Communication is not limited simply to telling subordinates what to do, and it is more than listening to instructions from superiors. Communication involves many interested parties, including ownership groups, those with a financial interest such as lenders, members of management, suppliers, customers, strategic partners, and, finally and most significant, employees at all levels. Part of the challenge of effective communication is the need to address the interests and needs for information presented by every stakeholder group. But this universal dependence on communication illustrates the importance of acquiring communication skills and exercising them to build sustainable business success.

TRAITS OF BAD COMMUNICATION

One of the most obvious examples of such a destructive break-down is what I call *triangular communication*. This scheme is commonly found in closely held enterprises, where a single individual has a good deal of power but is also subject to other influences, including those outside the organization. For instance, a company may be owned and led by a founder who has a history of conflict with a long-term subordinate executive or family heir. Their communication may degrade to a state where these two headstrong individuals, each accustomed to having his way, become engaged in endless bad-mouthing and unproductive arguing with one another, often with raised voices. If communication is bad enough between these two, they may decide it's best not to communicate directly at all—very much like a troubled marriage.

At this point a communication triangle often emerges. A third person enters as the go-between, charged with carrying messages between the two to avoid any one-to-one contact between them. This third person may be a spouse, a relative, another manager, or even a mutual friend. It's not important who it is; the problem is that the messenger exists at all.

Avoiding direct communication means that these two executives have, in effect, delegated power to someone else, whether they realize it or not. Because the go-between can present each of the others' words and desires, the go-between can control the message. Only a highly trained and ethical go-between is able to recognize, and then refrain, from putting a self-benefiting spin on their messages. Even if the go-between in the triangle is successful in behaving honorably, the chance for honest mistakes and errors is very high. Although the go-between may have good intentions to help, quite often the exact opposite occurs, and they end up in a negative light by both parties—a no-win position.

Triangular communication is an example of poorly developed communication skills, and even if it was appropriate and effective in grade school when we were learning how to communicate, it has no place in an economically driven business.

Although triangular communication and its effects provide a common and serious example of poor communication, it's far from being the only or even most severe problem. Semantic mismatch, for example, is a near universal obstacle. Semantic mismatch occurs when you think you're saying one thing and the person listening, while hearing the words clearly, applies another meaning. An example of this mismatch is a senior executive reminding a manager that quarterly performance reviews are due next week. To the executive, this may be a bland remark, something uttered to pass the time while waiting for a meeting to start. To a manager whose last set of performance reviews were followed by a demand to lay off a sizable portion of his department, however, the executive's pronouncement may resonate like the crack of doom. The only way to deal with semantic mismatch is to watch for unexpected reactions to things you have said and then try to determine what is causing the reaction.

As linguist Suzette Haden Elgin writes in *The Gentle Art of Verbal Self-Defense at Work,* "When the behavior of people who share your language seems bizarre or incomprehensible or completely unlike your expectations—and you have no reason to believe they have lost their minds—you should assume that there is a semantic mismatch." Once you have identified the key phrase, in this case *performance reviews,* you can find a nonthreatening way to explain precisely how you meant the term.

Even more problems can arise. For instance, anxiety and stress develop without good bottom-to-top communication. This problem is common when management and employees are cut off from one another, either physically or through unspoken rules.

In addition to preventing the completion of work, ineffective communication also causes wasteful duplication of effort. This problem is generic in rapidly expanding organizations, where left hand and right hand problems frequently occur. Size doesn't matter, as even small firms are not immune.

Perhaps even worse than duplication of effort is the phenomenon of contradicting initiatives. In a simple but serious example, while one part of a client company was preparing to mount a discount sale, another unit was retooling the firm's image as a premium-priced vendor. Such contradictory initiatives not only wasted effort but also caused harm, as customers became confused. Customers don't like to be confused.

The psychological aspect of poor communications is also important. When a company lacks clarity, its employees become confused, and their confusion usually transfers to customers. Without the communication of corporate goals and practices, employees are not clear about what the company stands for. Confused employees are, as a rule, inefficient. Of course, information, like nature, abhors a vacuum, so where poor communication fails to provide official information, the grapevine will infallibly provide it with its particular brand of gossip, rumor, and misinformation.

ACTION ITEM 1

Good leadership is all about clear communication.

Leadership must communicate three concepts—where the company is headed, what everyone needs to do to help get us there, and what is in it for them. We all listen to broadcasts over the WIFM station—What's in It For Me.

The consequence for companies that communicate poorly is that, when the staff lacks accurate and up-to-date information from leadership, it will turn to inaccurate and exaggerated grapevine-born rumor. As a result, when an easily foreseen crisis hits, leadership is caught by surprise. While surprises may be fun at birthday parties, they have no place in business. Limiting the flow of information, intentionally or unintentionally, always produces surprises, which are bad in the long run.

One case with which I am keenly familiar involved a small construction service company during the 2001 economic downturn. Accounts receivable and collections slowed and, by the time I came on the scene, more than $600,000 in receivables were at least 120 days past due. By that time, due to the delay and the likely bankruptcy of some of the company's customers, much of those overdue receivables were not collectible. Because of a simple failure to communicate the problem—a slowing rate of collections—to the CEO in time for corrective action, this surprise placed the future of the company into doubt.

TRAITS OF GOOD COMMUNICATION

Communication encompasses everything from the terms you use to explain last quarter's results to the board of directors to the expression on your face when employees say good morning. It consists of acts and words, and the way your communication is perceived is far more important than the way you intend it. While this book is not about the art of nonverbal communication or public speaking, a broad topic in itself, we can make some useful generalizations.

To begin with, good communication never attempts to catch people off-guard. The rule is: no surprises. The aim of business communication is to ensure that people who need to know about developments are informed in time to react or, more effectively, proact. The goal of communication is to express, not impress.

ACTION ITEM 2

Make sure that people who need to know about important developments are informed in time to react. Good communication means no surprises.

To endure, communication must be two-way. In a robustly communicating company, information flows up as well as down so that employees and managers are kept informed of developments throughout the company.

This means employees must feel free to ask questions. Don't just assume that if anybody had anything to tell you, they would. Managers must be seen giving their approval to two-way communication. As part of leadership, solicit input. Show by your actions that the practice of questioning is accepted and approved.

ACTION ITEM 3

Solicit input as well as providing it. Effective communication must be two-way.

Too often, communication within a company is left to its own devices in the mistaken assumption that it occurs naturally. Good communication is never an accident, nor does it occur of its own accord. In those environments where communication has denigrated to the point where discussion and agreement on important matters are basically impossible, I suggest creating a *Code of Conduct*. A Code of Conduct is nothing more than an agreement, among all relevant parties, to communicate and act according to a set of mutually agreed upon rules. Typical of every code are rules such as: we will not interrupt; we will focus on the problem, issue, or behavior; we will only speak for ourselves and not others; we will practice active listening; we will not use loud voices or sarcasm; all cell phones and pagers off; and we agree to use body language and eye contact that promotes respect.

The most important aspect of a Code of Conduct is that each one is created and tailored to each individual management or owner-ship team. One size does not fit all. Everybody involved in the meeting must have input into the code's creation for it to serve as a guide for effective communication.

Communication policies in successful companies are clear and consistent. Spell out communication practices in the company's manual to give official sanction to two-way communication. Then make sure that everyone understands the company's desired com-munication practice, that they are confident in speaking out as nec-essary, and that they will receive information relevant to their jobs.

ACTION ITEM 4

Spell out communication practices in the company's manual, and see that they are followed.

In every successful company, the important messages are put in writing. Messages relating to matters such as promotions, changes in compensation, employment contracts, commendations, and other personnel matters, as well as material events of any kind, are too important to depend solely on oral communication. Bulletin boards, company newsletters, even intraoffice e-mail and voice mail systems are all effective means of communication and are too often overlooked.

ACTION ITEM 5

Commit important communications to writing, using official documents and even legal forms if necessary.

Limits of Communication

Effective communication does not necessarily mean positive communication. In fact, often the most essential communication is of unwelcome or challenging news. Although each of us may use personal tricks to ease our discomfort when sharing bad news, this communication still isn't any fun. Henry Gilchrist, senior partner at one of the country's leading law firms, Jenkens & Gilchrist, has been training new lawyers for over 50 years. He tells his protégés never to delay bad news because it only gets worse with age. This is good advice.

Communication may look like a panacea for almost any problem, and it nearly is. But it's not easy and it's not perfect, and it's not even always possible. Communicating bad news always involves associating yourself with that bad news—on one end or the other—and the often unconscious urge to kill the messenger is a common result. There's no way to completely escape this, any more than to prepare people to hear bad news. However, using some techniques can mitigate the impact.

ACTION ITEM 6

Don't delay if you are planning a meeting to relay bad news. The sooner you act to stall rumors and calm fears, the better.

First, don't delay. The worse the news, the sooner people need to know. But don't move until you have double and triple checked the situation. Once you have the facts, mentally run through any questions, including hostile, defensive, or emotional ones that are likely to surface from the people receiving the unwelcome report. While you're at it, think about the likely feelings of these people. Uncomfortable as it may be, always deliver bad news face-to-face if possible.

Even if you're not the bearer of bad tidings, rarely will you find your message received equally well by all listeners. Even the best communication skills won't resolve all differences. So you must expect a certain level of dissent.

The belief that everything needs to be shared is tempting. But don't do it. Personnel issues, sensitive corporate information about mergers and acquisitions, and plans for new products and markets should be disseminated on a need-to-know basis. It is important to strike a balance between secrecy and openness when the right to privacy, competitive advantage, and the responsibility to shareholders are considered. Sharing everything with everybody is unnecessary, and many sound reasons may dictate that you should not.

One reason to keep talk under control is that too much talk can amount to too little communication. Engineers use a measure called the signal-to-noise ratio to describe how effectively a channel keeps extraneous interference from overwhelming the signals transmitted on the line. More generally, noise is anything that keeps a message from clear transmission. In the same way, superfluous communication about unimportant or irrelevant matters can hamper the clarity of important messages. Best to keep your communication under control; don't make the mistake of thinking more is better.

The grapevine, that annoying, unofficial scuttlebutt that seems to fuel anxiety, can create problems in a company when misinformation is distributed without countering official information. Make no mistake: you can't uproot the grapevine. You can only complement it and, to a limited extent, control it. One way to deal with the grapevine is to ensure that rumors aren't the only source of information. When, or preferably before, rumors start flying, preempt them with comprehensive facts disseminated through official communication channels.

Controlling the grapevine is trickier. The best way, which will require constant attention and finesse, is to embed your corporate culture within the grapevine itself by stocking it with company history and lore. Disseminate such stories to people you know are well connected through informal channels. The legends will take root, and their presence in the grapevine will help shape the discourse, giving it a far more positive aspect than if left on its own.

Finally, accept that while "no surprise" is the goal of effective business communication, even the healthiest builder of long-term value inevitably will be surprised. Management guru Peter Drucker said this about communication: "What the subordinate comes up with is rarely what the superior expects." So don't be surprised when you are surprised. If you work toward the goal of no-surprises communication, while keeping in mind that some surprises are beyond control, you will go a long way toward building long-lasting success in your company.

MAKING COMMUNICATION CENTRAL

General principles are fine when it comes to communication, but at some point these principles must translate into practical action. The first step is to conduct a communication survey or inventory. A communication inventory is simply an attempt to determine how effective communication and the flow of information, or lack thereof, is viewed throughout the organization.

Before conducting such a survey, be certain you really want the information. Many CEOs and managers are not interested in the truth if it shows them in an ugly light. What many seek is validation that they are already running a great company. They go through the motions of establishing better communication, when really they think matters are just fine as they are. They give orders and employees do as they're told. If the company has a problem, it's because employees are not carrying out orders effectively. Such an approach to management is all too common and in the end self-defeating. The CEO and senior managers must genuinely want to know what is taking place and must not be looking for phony results to validate what they are already doing.

To improve the odds that the collected data will be truthful and useful, you will need an independent outsider to create and manage the survey and presentation of the results. At minimum, a communication survey should address the following ten questions:

1. Do people know the official organization chart/structure?

2. Do employees know the company goals as well as their department objectives?

3. Do all employees know what is expected of them (job description)?

4. Do employees understand how their performance is measured?

5. Do employees know and understand the company mission, values, or vision statements?

6. Do employees have confidence in their leadership?

7. Do employees believe that personal matters will remain confidential?

8. Has each employee received, studied, and understand the employee handbook?

9. How do employees rate communication among each other and with management?

10. How do employees rate overall company morale?

A comprehensive survey might have more questions spun off these basic issues, but the results of every employee communications survey should determine what you're doing right and wrong, and how you can improve.

ACTION ITEM 7

Do a communications inventory to find out where you stand before embarking on a campaign to improve communications.

Making Communications a Priority

The only way you will ever be able to use the results from a communication inventory is to make communication a top priority throughout your organization. Unfortunately, if you are like most people, you probably already have a large number of priorities. Even if your desk is relatively clear at the moment, improving communication is a long-term commitment and requires much attention to detail. This long-term commitment is worthwhile. It will be a key contributor to long-term success.

With your survey in hand, establish a formal plan for communication. The plan can range from the very sophisticated to the perfectly simple. Your plan may include any or all of the numerous options, including an official ombudsman, bulletin boards, employee handbooks, internal memos, sophisticated intranets and e-mails, staff meetings, formal meetings with employee representatives, and casual hallway chats with donuts and coffee.

Improving communication throughout your organization is limited only by your ability to conceive of ways to speak and listen to stakeholders. It should reflect your company's special situation. Some things, however, are essential.

First, you must use some method of explaining important decisions to the people affected. Fiats mysteriously handed down from on high worked for the Olympian gods, but ordinary mortals have to hear it, read it, and see it. People want to know the thinking behind the latest developments.

Second, you must make provisions for face-to-face meetings. Electronic communication is marvelous, as well as highly addictive, but it is no substitute for sitting down across a table or even standing up in an auditorium and engaging in direct interaction.

ACTION ITEM 8

You have to make communication a priority if you expect it to be a tool that works for you instead of against you.

PORTRAIT OF SUCCESS

Warren Buffett

Warren Buffett is known as a great investor—possibly one of the greatest. Some say, however, he was not a great communicator. But perhaps Buffett should be reconsidered, not only for getting a return on a dollar but also for his skill at conveying ideas and information. To support this contention and the idea that communication is a fundamental business skill, consider the annual meeting of Berkshire Hathaway, the holding company for Buffett's diverse portfolio of investments.

If you've ever been to a public company's annual meeting, you know that the vast majority are dull, routine, sparsely attended affairs. Yet Berkshire Hathaway's meetings, guided by Buffett, have become so famous that an award-winning documentary movie, *Woodstock for Capitalists,* was made about them. Each spring for years, investors from around the globe have descended on Omaha, Nebraska, to hear the folksy insights from the Sage of Omaha, as he's known. In recent years, more than 15,000 people have attended, making Berkshire's annual shareholder meeting the largest in the world.

Why do they come? It's certainly not the extravagance of the ambience. Berkshire Hathaway and Buffett himself, as well as

Buffett's partner Charlie Munger, are famously frugal and unostentatious. In keeping with that message, for many years the meetings were held in the basement of an insurance company building. In the 1980s, they were moved to a hall of the Joslyn Art Museum, and today, because of attendance numbers, the meeting is conducted in the Omaha Civic Auditorium.

The weekend is full of typical, middle American activities to keep shareholders busy, including games of the baseball team Buffett owns—he throws out the first pitch. Companies in which Berkshire Hathaway has investments or special interests put on exhibits. These include Acme Brick, Benjamin Moore Paint, Coca-Cola, Dairy Queen, GEICO Insurance, Kirby (the vacuum cleaner company), See's Candies, and World Book Encyclopedia. Gorat's Steakhouse offers shareholders discounted meals.

But people really come to hear Buffett hold forth on the economy, investing, and just about any other topic that comes to his mind. He may offer wisdom on spotting the likely loser in a poker game: "If you look around and can't see who the patsy is, that's 'cause it's you." He may tell a tale about a man who was perplexed when he was bitten by a dog, after inquiring of a man standing next to the animal whether his dog would bite. "It ain't my dog," the ostensible owner responded.

Buffett's remarks on matters directly relevant to the company are almost an afterthought. It's the image, the style, the atmosphere of Nebraska and the Civic Auditorium and the Dairy Queen that Buffett is communicating—very effectively. Here's what one investor and regular attendee interviewed in *Woodstock for Capitalists* had to say: "Even though the principles don't change and the information's not new, it's really good once a year to spend five hours with Charlie and Warren and get the gyro back in sync and to resist a 23-year-old analyst yap, yap, yapping in your ear and to resist the fax that comes in every morning and says a lot of crap."

My grandfather, Olan Mills, impressed upon me the absolute importance of face-to-face communication. When I was young, he was always on the road, visiting locations and spending time with employees. I took this lesson to heart, so much so that when I was an Olan Mills executive in charge of more than 1,000 locations, I traveled a portion of 47 weeks each year just to stay in front of employees and to listen to their concerns. If you are in a leadership role, presenting yourself to stakeholders, especially employees, is critical to communicate values and culture. I believe strongly that communication is greatly enhanced by face-to-face encounters.

Additionally, face-to-face meetings are important for encouraging people to identify with a group. You can transmit large amounts of data effectively by sending Excel spreadsheets as e-mail attachments, but this medium has virtually no identity benefit. If you want people to see themselves as stakeholders with something to gain or lose from their firm's success or failure, they will need, from time to time, to see each other in person. For proof, just ask an absentee manager.

Who are stakeholders? They include shareholders, partners, beneficial owners such as family members, employees, customers, suppliers, and in some cases governing authorities. Each of these groups needs to have its own kind of meeting. For instance, family business owners often establish a family council. Family councils are basically a gathering of the family ownership group, including spouses, in-laws, and adult children. The goal of the council is to bring everyone together to communicate, educate, and make decisions on matters related to the business. As an added benefit, council meetings are typically held at venues with activities for the council group to coalesce. Although these meetings are both work and play, they are also the setting for big questions and decisions. Do we sell, bring in partners, or recapitalize? What is our hiring and termination policy for family members?

The dynamics of family business meetings mean they have special requirements. For instance, if the leaders of the family and the business are two different people, meetings are best held on neutral ground—not at the business where the CEO may wield outsized influence, nor in the family home where the patriarch or matriarch is on his or her own turf. Neutral ground encourages nonleaders to participate without unnecessary pressure from the physical environment.

The locale can even have a lingering affect. Meetings of the family owners of an East Coast fast-food chain were all held in the family home. After the dynamic patriarch who founded the business died, the practice continued. But in his absence, the meetings distinctly lacked action. I was called in to help with management succession, and after several meetings, it became obvious that council members were reluctant to voice opposition to any idea that they thought the founder might have disliked. We changed the venue, and council members moved outside the shadow of the founder to become a group of independent-minded yet cohesive forward thinkers. The atmosphere immediately lightened, and members were finally able to analyze the past and question the future.

Employee meetings, clearly, are entirely different affairs. These are generally held to inform, to motivate, and to lead rather than seek consensus or establish strategic direction. Customer meetings are likewise aimed at telling others about company products and plans. Leadership focused on long-term success will consider input from employees and customers essential and will establish multiple opportunities for customers to participate in product delivery. This will include focus groups, face-to-face interviews, questionnaires, and informal conversations.

Leaders meet with suppliers for many reasons, including discussing ways to cut costs, to speed delivery time, and to improve quality. Each of these encounters is an opportunity to build community, increase identification, improve communication, and lay the foundation for prolonged prosperity.

General guidelines apply to gaining value from any meeting. First, you must clearly understand why you are having the meeting. Do not ever just hold a meeting because "that's what we do." Always have a purpose and, following the leadership rule of no surprises, always tell participants ahead of time what the purpose and topic are. Don't try to force an agenda when there may, in fact, not be much of one.

ACTION ITEM 9

The first thing to know about any meeting is why you are having it. That understanding will guide further decisions about the time and location and who should attend.

The purpose of the meeting will tell you who should be there. For instance, if you're holding the meeting to announce a new product, you'll want to invite customers who might be in the market for just such a product. Because you probably won't be able to bring in all your customers, you may limit invitations to those whose budgets for purchasing your product exceed a certain threshold. You will likely have a budget for holding your meeting, which will also limit the number of attendees.

Once you know how many and what type of people will attend, select an appropriate venue. Meetings with owners of closely held firms, as discussed above, are often held in neutral locations. Employee meetings generally occur in company auditoriums or lunchrooms, because that's where the employees are and travel and time away from production is minimized. Some employee meetings, however, are convened in resort locations as an incentive to high achievers. Customer meetings are also sometimes held in resort locations, to encourage attendance and make a favorable impression. If you want business relationships to flourish over long periods, be certain to provide a congenial environment for meetings.

Timing is also an issue. If your meeting is intended to transmit bad news or to quell destructive rumors, then the basic rule is: the sooner, the better. But other meetings can be scheduled with more flexibility. Annual meetings, by definition, occur once a year, but you still have to decide on the day and the hour they'll take place. A meeting during work hours is probably the most convenient for employees and will draw the best attendance, but it may cause a productivity loss. The best general advice is to survey key attendees and participants and then schedule around them.

When the meeting is over, the job of making the most out of it has only begun. Follow up with attendees to determine if the meeting accomplished the stated purpose. Are they satisfied, and do they understand the outcome? Did they feel their input was taken into account and their questions answered?

Always come away from a meeting with follow-up action items in writing. This simple step will ensure that attendees participate and have some ownership of the outcome. Knowing how attendees perceive a meeting will go a long way toward helping design future meetings.

KEEPING A CLEAR CHAIN OF COMMAND

Officially sanctioned meetings can't take the place of face-to-face communication. At least a few extracurricular communication channels, where information is exchanged outside of the familiar confines of work, are vital. These channels help address the problem of approaching the person with the biggest desk and the most executive assistants on that person's turf. Find occasions to meet someplace else. A gathering in a restaurant or even a private home can bring down fences, encourage discussion, and best of all cause a subordinate to feel special. I remember many 6:30 AM breakfasts with my grandfather, and later my uncle, where over biscuits, cream gravy, and grits we discussed the business of Olan Mills.

For some, however, alternate communication channels make it unclear who is in command and, in worse circumstances, even lead to triangular communication. It's essential that employees know who is in charge. At Olan Mills, Inc., there was never any question about who was in charge during the early days, a situation common when the founder is also CEO.

In the beginning, Olan Mills did have a partner, who cashed in his war bonds to provide capital to keep the fledgling operation alive. Unfortunately, this partner walked in his sleep and he walked out the third floor of a rooming house and died on the sidewalk below. Although the company continued to operate efficiently under my grandfather, had the chain of command not been clear to all personnel, key employees likely would have maneuvered inappropriately, to the detriment of the company.

ACTION ITEM 10

Clear up uncertain chains of command or risk confusion, inaction, and destructive struggles for control.

If you recall or have read of the immediate aftermath of President Ronald Reagan's wounding at the hands of a deranged gunman, you know of then Secretary of State Al Haig's infamous words on national television, "I am in control here." According to the U.S. Constitution, which governs the chain of succession in case the President is killed or disabled, Haig was considerably overstepping his authority. Behind the scenes, the Presidential advisors had urged him to say nothing. Haig's overreaching was fodder for comedians and served as a spark that upset the stability of the U.S. government at a crucial time. Companies lack the benefit of being managed under the auspices of the Constitution, so confusion over who is in charge can be a serious threat to long-term prosperity.

When who is in control is not clear, reactions will include confusion, lack of direction, inaction, and even an outright struggle for control. Clarity of control is important to family business leaders, partners of closely held firms, department heads, owners, and investor groups alike. This problem with control is especially common in closely held firms, where one person may serve as the business leader while another represents and serves the ownership group. The owner representative may wish to pass out jobs, ownership shares, dividends, and perquisites to secure the loyalty of the owners. This approach can create confusion or even conflict with the business leader as to the allocation of company resources.

The distribution of power among shareholders is often a dicey matter and one that requires great articulation and written clarity. Some partnership groups decide to base decision making on one vote per member, while alternatively other groups choose to follow ownership percentages. Unfortunately, neither strategy is perfect if a stalemate occurs. Now the communication of a previously established voting procedure is critical. The shifting allegiance of voting stock may make it nearly impossible to tell day-to-day who is in charge, based on ownership.

But ownership isn't the only way to map a chain of command. Sometimes leadership is based on charisma, sometimes on intimidation. Rarely, and best, leadership is based on genuine merit. In these successful firms, the person in charge is the one who deserves the role based on demonstrated ability to lead and make decisions most likely to benefit the business and its stakeholders.

Whatever the source of control, making it clear to employees is critical. One way to make it clear is by using the familiar organization chart (something that many smaller firms are reluctant to create). Although these charts rarely represent the informal, cross-departmental relationships that influence decision making, they provide everyone with clarity regarding reporting and command relationships.

In my work, I have often listened to business leaders go on and on about how they don't really care about their title. What these inexperienced leaders don't realize is that their title is important to all the other stakeholders of the firm. Employees and stakeholders want to know who is in charge.

On a related matter, open book management and transparent management are common catchphrases that relate to communication. Often, these terms describe companies that go to unusual lengths to share with many or all people information that was previously restricted to senior executives. Generally, I'm in favor of this approach with the understanding that different corporate cultures require different levels of openness—especially on matters such as compensation, proprietary product development, M&A activity, labor union activities, strategic plans, and confidential personnel issues.

In these situations, more communication is not necessarily better. If you're a riveting speaker like Zig Ziglar, you may command the long attention of an audience, but otherwise, you will gain by speaking less and listening more.

Effective communication will not take place in a hostile environment. If, for example, you are communicating the news that the company is closing a division and the management of that division becomes highly emotional, this is not the time for a lengthy explanation or to defend your action. Instead, be smart and defuse the tension. Delay the detailed conversation for half an hour, or until the next day, or even into the following week.

In emotionally charged or hostile environments, you may think you're communicating clearly, and you might well be, but your listeners are unlikely to be receiving your message. In that case, many questions will not be asked, and confusion will likely reign supreme. None of this is to say you should avoid speaking when it's necessary. If it's an emergency, you may have to communicate on demand. Just consider the possibility that some communication will improve if it takes place at another time.

Finally, in any company encouraging open communication, especially one that values the unvarnished truth, it is important to educate people to understand what they are being told. This is essential if you are trying to manage transparently or use open book management, both of which require sharing a certain amount of technical information, such as financial results, with people whose experiences may not have adequately equipped them to understand it. As the leader, find a way to communicate effectively to your audience. In other words, don't tell anybody anything before you educate them. Peter Drucker says the first question about any communication is whether or not the intended recipient is equipped to receive it.

TELL IT LIKE IT IS

You should not, in any circumstance, treat something as a secret simply because it is painful or unwelcome. Candor is to be encouraged. The bywords here are: tell it like it is, and they don't apply only to you. You should promote your desire for information that may be unpleasant but necessary, and encourage all leaders to break down their personal barriers. This is especially true of those who, by virtue of their positions as protégés, might be treated with deference and shielded from constructive, if painful, criticism.

ACTION ITEM 11

Act decisively to encourage people to tell you the unvarnished truth and to do the same to all managers, including up-and-comers, relatives, and others who may be seen as your protégé.

How can you encourage such an environment? Perhaps the most difficult circumstance for candid communication is when you are dealing with an anointed leader or scion of the company's founder. Employees can be quick to realize which people are likely to become their boss someday and to treat them accordingly today. Other people are fearful that the candid criticism of someone with the ear of the top brass may generate prejudice against them. What you end up with is somebody who, because of their last name or position as a protégé, never hears the straight story or receives honest feedback about his own strengths or weaknesses.

The best way to deal with this problem is to find someone who already has the confidence to speak plainly. Good choices include a long-time retainer, veteran employee, or outsider who is immune to the internal politics at your company. What these people have in common is a power base of their own that is separate from that wielded by a "fair-haired" one. They can speak plainly because they aren't afraid of the consequences.

Once you find such a person, assign them the duty of exploiting their unique position. Make them an advisor, mentor, protector, or custodian of the fast-track young buck. Inform them, if they don't already know, that they will be insulated from the possible negative affects of wounded pride, hurt feelings, and insulted self-image resulting from their candid advice and observations. Likewise, inform the person you want to mentor. Let them know what to expect, why, and what your expectations are as a result. Their response may tell you a lot about whether they are, in fact, a good choice for the executive suite in the future.

The designated truth-teller approach is easier and, in many cases, more effective than trying to encourage an entire workforce to speak up. But you can also employ a more broad-based technique, *360-degree feedback,* to provide candor to an otherwise protected person. This technique, when done anonymously and especially if it confirms an attitude held by the anointed one, will be seen as more valid than feedback from a single mentor.

Objective feedback of the sort previously described is an effective method for giving someone generalized input about her performance. I was fortunate to learn about 360 feedback early in my leadership development. For a brief period, I was assigned to report to a very senior manager who had the ear of the chairman. He repeatedly told me I was too demanding and that people bristled at me behind my back. In came anonymous 360 feedback that clearly indicated his claims about me were not shared by others. This feedback helped the two of us resolve our differences and, more importantly, because of this experience, I became a firm believer in obtaining objective feedback and telling it like it is.

While you are at it, don't forget to provide objective opinions to one of the people most in need of them: You. If you are one of the senior leaders, to receive the most objective opinions, you must go outside the organization and seek help from outside directors, consultants, colleagues, and possibly competitors. Qualified outside opinions help in a number of ways by allowing you to see better both the forest and the trees, because they will offer perspectives different from anything you are likely to receive from inside the company. Ideas and opinions from outside can also crosspollinate in your mind, producing fruitful ideas filled with a hybrid vigor that would be impossible to obtain if you were relying only on fertilization from inside the company. I recommend executives participate in peer groups such as the Young President's Organization, Rotary, The Executive Council, Toastmasters, breakfast gatherings, or any other group that holds professional development as its primary purpose and provides insight from others that walk in similar shoes.

ENABLING TWO-WAY COMMUNICATION

Another essential trait of communication is that it be two-way. But two-way communication doesn't necessarily happen naturally or by itself. To jump-start it, you have to make yourself open to communication from people working at other levels, in other departments, and even in different organizations. This likely includes establishing an open-door policy, sponsoring face-to-face meetings, or printing your personal telephone number and e-mail address on a business card.

As the CEO and majority owner of a regional welding supply company, Randy Squibb insisted that all employees and customers have his home and mobile telephone numbers. He told me that, "I want those people who really do have a problem to call me whenever. Those who want to just chit-chat have been respectful of my personal time."

Don't stop by merely opening the door. Make sure people know what will await them if they walk through it. That means doing two things. First, use and reward employee ideas and suggestions. Nothing motivates people to offer constructive suggestions as much as the possibility that their ideas actually will be implemented. Next, add the prospect of significant financial or other rewards to that possibility, and you will go a long way toward assuring a steady flow of helpful ideas on improving performance from the people who know the work best.

My experience has certainly been that the best ideas are the ones born from the person doing the job. Photographing cranky babies and small children can be a real chore. Although Olan Mills is known for offering the highest quality photographs, it is really the customer experience that was the competitive advantage. A significant aspect of the experience was safety. Photographers, therefore, were instructed to never leave a child on a posing table unattended. In the early years, before a photographer would either raise or lower a backdrop, they were required to place each child on the floor. While it gave the customer the certainty Olan Mills's photographers took the safety of their child seriously, this practice was clearly both inefficient and cumbersome.

My cousin deserves the credit for solving the safety concern efficiently. Working as a photographer one summer during high school, he asked his father, the chairman, if it was possible to push a button to raise and lower the backdrops. Today such automation is commonplace, but in the late 70s this idea was novel.

The significance of this story is that many Olan Mills, Inc., photographers had probably thought of something similar but didn't have access to the chairman. As it was, the very valuable idea was implemented in every camera room in the company. If other employees had direct access to the chairman, the new backdrop system might have surfaced even sooner. What ideas for improvement are people in your organization secretly harboring?

Apply the rule that people will tend to support what they help to create. Then allow stakeholders to assume ownership for what they have created. A savvy CEO may have the idea, but he will implement the idea in a manner that allows others to share ownership, as though they were on the invention team. Sharing is fairly simple to accomplish, as the CEO may present the idea as one possibility and ask, "What do you think about this?" The employee approves of it and soon feels as though she's created it with you.

This operates in my field. I probably haven't faced a business problem when I didn't feel confident about saying, "Here's one answer." But instead, I direct my clients through the options and then help them pick the one that has the greatest likelihood of success. It also has the greatest ownership.

The second thing you have to do to encourage two-way communication is spare the messenger. The tendency to blame the bearer of bad tidings is age old. Resist it with all your might. Nothing chokes off the stream of information faster than the fear that the information may be unpleasing to a powerful recipient and that the messenger will be punished for delivering it. Some of your most valuable employees will be the ones who bring you bad news.

ACTION ITEM 12

Never punish people who bring you bad news, and always reward those who bring good ideas.

It's essential for any manager to be in possession of important negative news about events on her turf. If you don't know what's going on, especially when it may be bad for the company, you're not likely to promote sustained wealth building. If someone brings you bad news, avoid even the slightest taint of criticism towards the person delivering the message. Instead, praise and reward them. That way, you'll increase the chances of promptly hearing the next time a material event—good or bad—takes place.

One company I worked with was in the business of delivering prepared foods to convenience stores. The senior managers promoted someone inexperienced into the role of manager of the firm's all-important fleet of delivery trucks. This person failed to overcome some persistent difficulties in servicing the cab air conditioners in the trucks. As a result, the company, which was based in the Southwest, began experiencing significant losses of experienced drivers, who resigned rather than work in sweltering conditions. In one short period, 15 percent of the delivery employees resigned. The company's ability to fulfill its mission was significantly hampered, because these drivers had relationships with customers and specific experience in seeing to their needs.

The CEO clearly should have had this information. Although truck air conditioning might have been perceived as something so mundane as to be beneath the CEO's notice, its lack was plainly a material event striking at the heart of the business. Yet the CEO was not told, and the company suffered significant loss of business and damage to its long-term value.

How could this setback have been overcome? Well, first, only a qualified and experienced person should have been placed in such an important position. Failing that, the CEO should have made it clear that he was to be informed of any material event. He should have made it clear that bringing bad news was not a crime but a duty. Furthermore, a system to make it easy for the knowledgeable parties to pass on information should have been in place. This system doesn't have to be anything elaborate. A simple weekly or monthly meeting at which department heads report the status of their initiatives to the CEO would have provided an opportunity and a climate appropriate for passing on possibly unpleasant news. Furthermore, these meetings would have given the CEO a semi-public platform on which to demonstrate that messengers, no matter how bad their messages, would be rewarded rather than "shot."

WALKING THE TALK

This chapter began by saying that poor communication is a common problem. But quite often the problem is more subtle. Often, a business's leaders are ready and willing to receive communications, but they are not perceived to be that way. So they hear nothing, and they get unpleasant surprises. When they are the ones communicating, their information is perceived as unreliable or is not interpreted accurately by the recipients. In other words, perception is an all-important key to good communication. You must be perceived as open to listening and perceived as trustworthy to hear, before your communications will be effective.

How can you build confidence in your abilities and attitudes toward communication? Just talking about it won't do the job—you have to walk the talk. It's perhaps ironic that talking isn't enough to ensure good communication. But in the case of Newell Farms, actions—such as rewarding bearers of bad tidings or spending time visiting with shop-floor workers, are the only things that speak at all.

OUT OF FOCUS

Newell Farms

The founder of Newell Farms was a powerful, hard-driving, hard-drinking, violent man. His three sons, who inherited the $20 million agricultural industry company and ran it after their father's death, were laconic farmers. They were comfortable on a tractor seat but not behind a speaker's podium, not even in casual conversation. Not even with each other. Newell Farms was a communication-based disaster in the making almost as soon as the three brothers began trying to manage it together.

Part of the problem was that they're simply not verbal people. Not only do they not talk among themselves, but if you put them in a board meeting, they won't share 50 words all day. They may grunt to indicate assent or disagreement, but they don't say what's on their mind. They simply do not speak.

Part of this issue is situational. These businesspeople are outdoorsy, farmers. They don't talk much. The other part is that tremendous conflict exists among them. That is, they deliberately don't talk to each other. As a result, they have failed to wrestle with significant problems.

The primary issue that is left unresolved by the lack of communication is that, basically, they have huge differences in values. One brother wants to go out and borrow money to grow the business aggressively. The other is so conservative that he doesn't want to borrow a nickel.

The second issue is they have deep scars from alcoholism in their background. Specifically, the father was a shotgun-toting, abusive, in-your-face alcoholic. The kind of issue-avoiding, codependent behavior that is often seen in families of alcoholics is very much in evidence here. The result is a company that is almost paralyzed by lack of communication at its highest levels.

In particular, lack of communication has created an inability to agree on company mission, vision, and purpose. So there's a lack of leadership. Lack of leadership is the kiss of death in any organization. This is a business that grew 300 percent in just a few years. It became a leader in its industry. But rather than applauding that and recognizing the great efforts, they've become highly conflicted. With growth comes a greater demand for capital. Because the guys can't get together on a strategy on how to tap into fresh capital, they're a likely acquisition target.

Communication is never easy. You only have to look at almost any family or married couple to realize how difficult it can be. When it comes to building and maintaining a long lasting, wealth-building company, a determined effort is required to establish the right mixes of communication. The payoff will be enormous.

ACTION ITEMS

ACTION ITEM 1
Good leadership is all about clear communication.

ACTION ITEM 2
Make sure that people who need to know about important developments are informed in time to react. Good communication means no surprises.

ACTION ITEM 3
Solicit input as well as providing it. Effective communication must be two-way.

ACTION ITEM 4
Spell out communication practices in the company's manual, and see that they are followed.

ACTION ITEM 5
Commit important communications to writing, using official documents and even legal forms if necessary.

ACTION ITEM 6
Don't delay if you are planning a meeting to relay bad news. The sooner you act to stall rumors and calm fears, the better.

ACTION ITEM 7

Do a communications inventory to find out where you stand before embarking on a campaign to improve communications.

ACTION ITEM 8

You have to make communication a priority if you expect to be a tool that works for you instead of against you.

ACTION ITEM 9

The first thing to know about any meeting is why you are having it. That understanding will guide further decisions about the time and location and who should attend.

ACTION ITEM 10

Clear up uncertain chains of command or risk confusion, inaction, and destructive struggles for control.

ACTION ITEM 11

Act decisively to encourage people to tell you the unvarnished truth and to do the same to all managers, including up-and-comers, relatives, and others who may be seen as your protégés.

ACTION ITEM 12

Never punish people who bring you bad news, and always reward those who bring good ideas.

CHAPTER 6

The Journey of Passion and Balance

Passionate leadership is not about getting rich. If your mission is only to enrich yourself financially, you're passionate about something other than your business. Passionate business leaders, first and foremost, love what they do. Money is the by-product.

In *Making a Living, Making a Life*, author Mark Albion quotes a study conducted by Srully Blotnick that vividly demonstrates this point. Fifteen hundred business school students were divided into two groups, those that said they wanted to earn a lot of money now in order to do what they wanted later in life and those that wanted to follow their true interests from the start. Of the 1,500 graduates, 1,245 fell into the first group and only 255 were committed to pursuing their interests ahead of making money.

Guess what? Twenty years later 101 of these individuals achieved millionaire status. Surprising, however, 100 of these individuals came from the group of students that said they wanted to pursue their true interests and only 1 came from the group that essentially said making money was their primary goal.

You can see this validated by the activity of the world's most admired business executives. If it were all about the money and not about the fun and the passion, then would Bill Gates and Jack Welch continue to work? If it were just about money, why wouldn't the richest men in the world just go off and do something else? This passion is not confined to Gates and Welch. Another high-tech entrepreneur, Silicon Graphics and Netscape cofounder Jim Clark, certainly has plenty of money—he's a billionaire—but he still likes to find projects he's excited about and work passionately to see them realized. The same goes for countless other perhaps less well known but no less committed leaders of closely held businesses who have reached a comfortable level of security.

PORTRAIT OF SUCCESS

Williamson-Dickie

The smell of smoke lingered in the air and the fire engine's ruts were visible in the parking lot, still full of water expended to fight the blaze. Although the flames were out and firefighters had saved the closely held company's factory machinery as well as a good portion of the work in progress and inventory, the decision was already made.

The Latch Apparel Company had sewn its last garment. The company would be closed, the assets sold off, and the proceeds distributed to the owners. The problem? None of the later-generation owners cared enough to want to fight the necessary battles to keep the 50-year-old company in business.

Across town, events had gone differently for the Williamson-Dickie Manufacturing Co. The company hadn't experienced a destructive fire, but since 1922, when two Williamsons and a Dickie paid $12,500 for a Fort Worth overalls factory, the company and its owners had been forced to adjust to their fair share of turmoil. Difficult episodes included the making of far too many wild-hued painters's pants during the 1970s and, a decade before, detouring near-disastrously into polyester suits.

But Dickies, as the company is commonly known, navigated it all. America transformed from a blue-collar economy, where the clothes were as rugged as the unions, and entered the information age wearing, ironically, the same rugged work clothes that were the mainstay of the manufacturing era. Dickies survived a change that could have been disastrous had its utilitarian style not wound up fashionable. It even prospered with the emergence of the grunge trend.

Today, while Latch is a memory, Dickies sells hundreds of products and dominates the $1.6 billion market for branded work clothes. The company employs over 5,000 people in 28 plants and 7 countries from Japan to England.

What made the difference between Latch, whose owners were willing to give it all up after being burned out, and Dickies, whose owners weren't willing to give up at all? What kept Dickies going to produce revenues exceeding $500 million and emerge as the nation's top brand of work wear? The answer, in one word, is passion. Dickies survived while Latch didn't, because the leaders who ran Williamson-Dickie had a passion for the business.

Passion is why Philip Williamson, grandson of the founder, occupies the office of the chairman and CEO today. It's why he pays such close attention to the details of his products that he is said to be able to sew a pair of pants himself. It's why, although he is the third-generation scion of one of Texas's wealthiest families, he heads straight for the manufacturing floor of any Dickies plant he visits.

Love of the business keeps Williamson, and the company he heads, focused and stable. "It's probably because we have stayed with our core businesses and continued to focus on that," he says to explain the company's longevity. "Where there are opportunities that spin off our core business, we take advantage of those. But we always come back."

It's no exaggeration to say that the passionate desire of leaders, both present and future, to stay in the business is a primary force keeping many closely held firms alive. "That's the only thing that's allowed some companies in the industry to survive," says Ed Miller, CEO and son of the founder of H.L. Miller & Son, a small, closely held manufacturer in Iola, Kansas. "I've seen a lot of companies in the last several years fold up shop because times were tough and there wasn't any reason to carry on."

Sometimes the decision not to carry on is rendered moot by the failure of passionless leaders to do the minimum required for corporate survival. One client company, a $30 million maker of heavy industrial equipment, was run by the sons of the founder, a man who never hesitated to wade into the mud, fend off welding sparks, or grab the heavy end of a large box—he enjoyed being involved in all aspects of running the firm. The sons, however, were reluctant to dirty their Guccis. As a result, the firm drifted wildly without active leadership. The sons regarded the company as theirs to loot, not to lead, and on their way they ran out of money. Because the boys couldn't get out fast enough, the company was the product of a liquidation sale. Their problem: a lack of passion for their industry.

The leaders's passion often distinguishes a company that not only moves forward but also overtakes its rivals. Charismatic and celebrity entrepreneurs such as Richard Branson, Michael Dell, Bill Gates, and Herb Kelleher dominate intensely competitive markets, because exceptional people are drawn to the exceptionally powerful business visions these leaders so passionately project. They have passion for their businesses and their work, versus a mere passion for financial reward. To them, business is a competition, and they're passionate about winning.

Passion plays a key role in helping leaders innovate. Passion allows and, indeed, drives people to think creatively. Passionate leaders think about the business all the time. From constant mental application comes innovation.

Olan Mills was very passionate, and he transmitted passion to his son, who leads the company today. Olan Mills II, with whom I worked for many years, was renowned for his knowledge of the company minutiae. He could take someone on a tour of the operations and explain details of almost every person's job in the facility. As he walked through the facility, employees at all levels would approach with questions about their jobs. He was referred to, kindly, as "a kid in a candy store" when he explained operations. It was true, it was sincere, and it was a result of the genuine passion he felt for leading innovation in a photography company.

Passion is even more important (critical) in a start-up firm. When a leader has direct contact with a large portion of a workforce, exhibiting passion can make a huge difference in morale. Few small companies can afford to hire top talent. Even if the leaders lack the charisma to draw people to them by sheer strength of personality, they can still motivate employees to work as hard and stay as late as workers do at even the richest companies. Leaders accomplish this by exhibiting personal passion—by showing it—like Richard Branson, Michael Dell, and Bill Gates.

Let's be clear. I'm not talking about either charisma or celebrity. Charisma is not required to become a successful long-term leader. Passion is not the same as charisma. We don't need training in Shakespearean theatrics to experience and to show passion. The point is that if you are not conveying a message that says, "I'd rather be here talking to you about our company than anyplace else in the world," then you may not be feeling and revealing your passion for this business. In other words, employees can read your heart.

Manufacturing passion sounds like mass-producing love— impossible. Passion, our society holds, has to come by itself or is worthless, and that viewpoint has something to it. No business leader can simply ordain passion. Yet something is producing the passion in business leaders who succeed long term. If you look for them, you'll find clear similarities among passionate leaders.

Before a firm can generate passion, it must permit it to exist. That's not as easy as it may sound. Passion is sometimes considered a prelude to poor judgement. A criminal judge who determines that a crime was committed in the heat of passion may reduce the charge or penalty, even if the act was murder. The idea is that passion can keep people from being mentally capable of knowing what they are doing or from discerning right from wrong. On the other hand, passion can also unleash creativity. Firms wishing to encourage an ardent desire for business success have to get rid of the negative interpretation of passion.

Parents rarely have any trouble developing passionately strong feelings for their offspring. Founders of companies will likely be disappointed if they expect the next generation of leaders to bear the same affection for their company. Business leaders can increase the odds that those who follow will develop a nearly equal enthusiasm for the business—if they expose them to the satisfaction, the heart, of the business at an early age.

Dickies's CEO, Phillip Williamson, says some of his earliest memories are of accompanying his father into noisy, bustling garment factories. He worked at the company part-time and summers during high school. The energetic clamor made an enduring impact. After college, he returned to the company, where he has worked ever since.

Long-lived businesses maintain what can best be called a family atmosphere. The Haggar Apparel Co. grew into one of the largest closely held companies in the United States without sacrificing the family feeling, according to Joe M. Haggar III, CEO of the company his grandfather started. Many Haggars worked at the company over the years, and Haggar says that those who were not related by genes or marriage were included in the extended clan. That's true today, even though Haggar is now publicly owned. "I still consider a lot of other people here part of the family," says Haggar. "And we still consider ourselves as having a family spirit."

Passion-driven businesses carefully manage the indoctrination of next generation leaders. Those who are able to sustain passion report that they downplay the negative aspects of working at the business and emphasize the positive parts. That may seem superficial. Yet portraying involvement in the business as an enjoyable activity from the first exposure on can have a powerful and positive long-term effect.

Even the smallest businesses can become relatively complex systems. They involve many tasks, functions, skills, and responsibilities, ranging from the board chairman emeritus to the newest mailroom clerk. Imparting the big picture of complexity is not always easy, especially for a veteran company founder who understands almost intuitively the structure and interplay of all the company's parts.

Unlike Legos, you can't tear a company down and rebuild it just to show latecomers how it was assembled. Many scions of business have gained deep knowledge of their company's workings by the simple means of filling a wide array of duties at the firm. Few methods are superior to time spent in marketing, followed by operations, followed by finance, etc. as preparation for eventual entry into the executive suite.

An important added benefit of rotating designated future leaders through a variety of jobs is that it provides them with a better chance of finding an aspect they truly love. Heidi Viramontes's first job at International Garment Processors was on the plant floor. After working her way up the ranks, she is now president of the 450-employee El Paso commercial laundry her father founded, and because of the love she has shown for the business, she will take over the chairman's job when her father retires. "She's the one who's been most involved, and she knows the business better than any of the other children," founder Cesar Viramontes explains.

The idea that offspring of founders should come in at the top is an outdated one—if, indeed, it ever had any real validity. In the same way, the idea that only sons should be encouraged to develop an enthusiasm for business is similarly inappropriate in this day. The fact that many daughters are walking successfully in a parent's shoes is evidence that females are just as likely to possess business acumen as males. In fact, a large body of evidence suggest that female executives are better equipped to handle differences. Women who rise and become executives do so in spite of overwhelming odds against male competition. Many have learned that rather than fighting this opposition head on, it is better to negotiate, bring people together, and develop and focus on common goals. In this regard, many women are better equipped to handle the differing opinions that frequently arise in companies.

The founder of the famous King Ranch, Richard King, had two sons and three daughters. Only one, Alice King, decided to follow her father into the family business. The five children from her marriage to Robert Kleberg owned the vast cattle operation equally until 1954, more than a century after its founding. Yet, despite the debt the King Ranch owed to Alice King, even this business failed to appreciate women. According to Sally Kleberg, a fifth-generation descendant of Richard King, "I found that in my family, the women were expected to be educated, to be supportive, and to pull their own weight. But not to rock the boat."

Gender discrimination in business today is still unfortunately widespread, despite the fact that it is at best a waste of potential to deny an interested girl the opportunity to develop and display her passion for business. Heidi Viramontes is the second of Cesar Viramontes's eight children, but she's the sole heir apparent for good reason. According to her father, the experience she gained working in that low-level job and many others at the company amply prepared her for the responsibility. "She's the most qualified," he says, "and no one questions her ability."

Passion-producing activities can extend well into the public sphere. Public promotion of a firm's image inculcates corporate pride in organization members as well as in the general populace. At Dickies, for instance, press releases trumpet that Henry Fonda wore Dickies in *The Grapes of Wrath*, that cast members of *ER* wear the clothes, that Dickies don the Texas State Fair's gargantuan Big Tex sculpture—waist 285 inches, inseam 185. Pop musicians such as Hootie and the Blowfish have donned Dickies, and the company's headquarters is in a renovated school, the same attended by Ginger Rogers as a Fort Worth high school student. In addition to achieving marketing goals, public proclamations of a private company's special accomplishments promote passion among all employees and inspire them.

ACTION ITEM 1

Inculcating passion isn't enough. Any business must be financially successful to justify its own existence. It does no one any good to devote genius and inspiration to a commercial enterprise that is not commercially viable.

Going beyond passionate means, among other things, running the business as more than a private employment agency dedicated to providing lifetime job security to members of the club. This applies especially to jobs that provide rich salaries in return for little work. One problem with a lifetime sinecure is that it removes the element of risk that must be present to inspire the imagination. If nothing is to be gained, nothing will be ventured. At the same time, giving those who are part of the club ironbound employment contracts discourages talented, nonanointed employees from sticking around. With the writing on the wall plainly visible, they can read that their future promotions will be limited to the openings the heirs choose to vacate.

In addition to serving as job banks, closely held businesses are sometimes seen more as vehicles for the preservation of wealth than as ongoing enterprises. Businesses are somewhat like bicycles: it is far easier to keep them upright if they are moving forward. Considerable evidence shows that the pace of change is accelerating today—the bike path is getting bumpier. Businesses that act too conservatively, parking on top of their wealth like stalled bicyclists, are likely to find themselves being passed by more enterprising competitors.

While nothing is wrong with accumulating wealth, when wealth is the only end, its accumulation can prove disappointing, even corrosive. Many a successful business founder has taken care to raise offspring with all the wealth-based advantages the founder lacked, only to find that none of the next generation is interested in investing any energy and time into the business that created the wealth. King Ranch founder Richard King's experience, when four of five children declined to follow him into the family business, is far from unusual.

One way to get around the problems created by business success is to make sure that something other than just the creation of wealth gets attention. The Levi Strauss Company, for example, has become highly respected for its insistence on quality since the founder began selling jeans to Gold Rush miners in 1873. Their mantra of quality has long overshadowed mere financial return.

It's not enough to set high standards for a firm. Fast-track future leaders must be asked and expected to excel in their own right and to make their own contribution. Heidi Viramontes recalls her first day on the job at International Garment Processors. When the 19-year-old novice failed to make her quota, her father was unsympathetic. She recalls him saying, "How many did you do? That's all?" Rather than feeling dejected, the young Viramontes responded with passion, thinking, "I'll show him."

In addition to stressing product quality and productivity, simple pride of ownership can also ignite passion. Gertrude Boyle, cofounder of Columbia Sportswear Co. in Portland, Oregon, has become a familiar public figure from her appearances in the company's advertisements. She repeated this message to her son Tim: "You can't have just anyone take over the responsibility of running your company." Boyle explains, "It's very important for future generations to remain involved." Tim is now president and CEO of the family-controlled firm.

Public companies almost always consider rewarding shareholders with profits, dividends, and stock price the highest goal. But what's best for employees and communities may be equally important to closely held firms. Levi has shown the world how to be a responsible—and successful—manufacturer in communities of the developing world. Meanwhile, publicly owned companies such as Nike have been embarrassed by the poor working conditions reported in many of its factories. Closer to home, many closely held firms have kept jobs in U.S. factories when other companies might have exported them to exploit cheap labor.

ACTION ITEM 2

Stressing what's best for employees and communities as well as owners can transform an enterprise from a business into a higher calling.

In her 1997 book, *The Stewardship of Private Wealth*, Sally Kleberg writes of the importance of looking at a business as more than just a commercial concern. "From its inception, the King Ranch was built on the vision of being stewards of the land, the people, the expertise, the community, and the world," she says. "Descendants were taught to believe that stewardship should be thoughtful, wise, effective, and committed to the next generation." This appeal is precisely the sort that encourages passion. Specific moves that call people to a higher mission include corporate support of worthy causes, creating and building traditions, and a mission or vision that appeals to a more universal spirit than merely padding shareholder value.

Think about, for example, the "Three Basic Beliefs" Sam Walton established in 1962: (1) Respect for the Individual, (2) Service to Our Customers, and (3) Strive for Excellence. All levels can relate to these ideals. They carry the added benefit of firing people up— very important. A statement such as, "Our prime goal is to increase shareholder value," may sound beautiful in the executive suite, but is lost, almost resented, on the shop floor. (How many factory employees leave work with the satisfaction of having contributed to increasing shareholder value?)

Perhaps the most basic passion-building move of all is to appeal to people's innate desire to create immortality by building something that will outlast them. When a greater cause or higher calling is given as the reason for perpetuating a business, it touches one of the deepest human needs. When forming Olan Mills, Inc., my grandfather led people with his vision for our company. That vision related to outstanding customer interaction. "Our first responsibility is to our customer. The success or failure of the company and the employees will be measured by the manner in which we meet our responsibilities to our customers, to the people with whom we do business, and to each other." It's clear, simple, and calls people to account for a higher principle than mere self-enrichment.

Leaders who don't have a genuine passion for what they do typically manage from a point of view that defines success as minimizing dissatisfaction. This is nothing more than the absence of complaints. Passionate leaders prefer to measure the performance of their business through the satisfaction and enthusiasm of customers. Consider measuring success by the customer's excitement level. Think of Harley Davidson, where tattoo counts are one measure of customer enthusiasm. Measuring business success by customer enthusiasm is entirely different than minimizing dissatisfaction via statistical controls.

Take Irish supermarket owner Fergal Quinn. Quinn, renowned as "Super Quinn" in his native land and elsewhere, offers a cash reward to any customer who brings in a shopping cart with a wobbly wheel. With this simple technique, he has turned one aspect of customer service over to customers. Ordinarily, of course, customers who pull a wobbly cart out of the line don't do anything other than put it aside, annoyed, and select another. A defective shopping cart may affect 10, 15, or more people every day, negating their shopping experience. Now Super Quinn's customers come in and test shopping carts, hoping to find one with a bad wheel. They take defective carts out of service immediately. Not only is Fergal Quinn's wobbly cart award program innovative, it clearly demonstrates leadership that not only wants to engender goodwill but create excitement and passion among customers. Will they love shopping in his stores? You bet!

These passion-building ploys should be more than mere tricks. If they are to work, current leaders of the business must embrace them as passionately as they hope later generations will. Whether it is Gert Boyle building pride of ownership in her son, or Phillip Williamson's father taking his child on tours of the plant, the leaders must embody passion for their business before they can expect other associates or customers to do the same.

Embodying passion is, of course, different from merely mimicking it. If leaders are to maintain passion, they should have the tools and perquisites to excel. As a senior Olan Mills executive, for instance, I could call up a $20 million corporate jet to transport me to a business meeting. There were business reasons for making this aircraft available to Olan Mills's management, but one of its most profound personal effects was to make me feel special, that my labors were acknowledged, and that the company where I worked knew I was making a contribution to its success.

ACTION ITEM 3

Providing appropriate perks to those who have earned them will go a long way toward building a corporate culture that makes those working at the business believe they would never dream of working elsewhere.

Passionate leaders make their business activities seem fun. They accomplish this, in part, by refraining from the usual complaints about the day at work when in front of leadership heirs or new employees.

None of these techniques guarantees passion. Passion can be encouraged, but it can't be forced. In fact, paradoxically, allowing people to find their passion elsewhere makes them more likely to discover that their true calling indeed lies within the business. Senior generations sometimes feel uncomfortable allowing a child to explore what they want in a career. But giving later generations the freedom to explore options ensures that a decision to go to work for the enterprise will, at the very least, be made of their own free will. After all, how much passion could you hold for somebody else's dream?

It worked for E.L. Miller, where the founder's grandson labored for several years in data processing before returning to the family firm, where he is now president. As Boyle says, "It is important that they make the decision about joining the company. It doesn't do anyone any good if they are forced into something they don't believe in."

Leaders have tried many means to keep later generations interested in the business, ranging from "golden handcuffs" employment agreements, which penalize an executive financially for an early departure, to authoritarian decrees. But those that work best work from the heart and are based on personal passion rather than proclamation. As Philip Williamson says, "Why did I stay in the business? I like it, and I like the action."

Now for the kicker. Passion alone isn't enough. Too much passion, unadulterated by balance, can in fact be a negative. Time and again, I run across businesses run by dedicated, disciplined, hardworking—and, yes, passionate—business leaders who put in 70-plus hour weeks, 52 weeks a year, for 20 or more years. In this way, they sometimes grind out remarkable success—or so it seems. It may take many years for the problems sown by this approach to appear, but they very often do, and they are frequently intractable. The saddest part is that they are usually easily avoidable, and the cure is actually pleasant.

What are these problems? Frequently, when their working lives are over, prematurely in many cases, these dedicated workers are surprised to find out that their families either don't know them or actively resent them. They have lived for their job; they have no friends or activities outside work to occupy their time, and without work they are profoundly unfulfilled. This realization may come too late—after the business has been sold or has failed, in retirement or, unfortunately, after the family has been torn to pieces.

OUT OF FOCUS

J. Paul Getty

J. Paul Getty is remembered as the richest American of his time and one of the richest men in the world from the end of World War II until his death in 1976. What is not commonly known is that his father was a self-made millionaire who, around the turn of the century, gave his son the essential start-up money for Getty Oil Company. The Getty Trust, eventually worth more than $1 billion and the source of the Getty fame, was, in fact, established by Getty's mother, Sarah. Getty's single-minded obsession throughout his long life was to outdo his father, and the means by which he kept score was the dollar value of his mother's trust.

Getty proved highly adept at making money, but he was less accomplished in virtually every other sphere of life. Working from hotel rooms and communicating with his far-flung business empire only by telephone, he avoided all normal association with people. He embarked on an orgy of thoughtless marriages in his late 20s and early 30s. Typically, weeklong courtships preceded marriages measured in months. From these five loveless unions came five neglected sons, each receiving the Getty name and, to varying degrees, some portion of the fortune.

Getty had little use for people and almost none for the possessions his wealth allowed him to acquire. This included even the famous Getty Museum, the most richly endowed private museum in the world. He never visited it. Instead, he had time only for his ledger sheets and mistresses.

Getty's life conspicuously lacked balance. It held no weekend trips to the countryside or seashore, no interests of any kind beyond business. Much the same was true for his all but forgotten children. His oldest son, George, descended into a nightmare of drugs and alcohol, ending his life at age 49. George's wife bluntly told reporters, "His father killed him."

Ronald, the second son, in a futile attempt to compete financially with his father throughout his life, ultimately had to file bankruptcy in 1992, listing no assets and debts in excess of $40 million. The third son, Paul Jr., was a heroin addict until middle age. He spent much of his adult life in treatment clinics. Fourth son Gordon was the most traditional, living with his wife in San Francisco, devoting himself to theoretical economics and to composing classical music. The youngest son, Timothy, tragically died during surgery at age 12. His father was too busy to be present. With the possible exception of Gordon, none of the Getty adult children found balance in their lives. Following in their paternal footsteps, they had few or no interests beyond self-destruction and self-indulgence.

After J. Paul Getty's death, members of the third generation examined the wreckage of the lives around them. Paul Jr.'s wife Talitha, companion of the ballet star Nureyev and darling of the paparazzi, had died of a drug overdose. His daughter by a first marriage, Aileen, was dying of AIDS. Jean Paul III had his ear cut off by his abductors during a kidnapping, and later lapsed into a coma of suspicious origin, and never fully recovered.

The wreckage of the Getty family was strewn about the lavish estates and five star hotels of Europe, England, and America. These heirs were determined to do something about their off-balance genes and took as their model the successful Rockefeller family. The Rockefellers had managed to combine fame, wealth, and individual accomplishments; so, too, would the Gettys.

In later years, rid of drugs, Paul Jr. at last found interests that gave meaning to his life. After receiving $750 million as his share of the Getty Trust, he became a major benefactor to his adopted country of England. He gave $20 million to preserve the British film legacy and another $50 million to the British National Gallery. For these and other gifts, he was appointed a Knight of the British Empire. He restored the historic estate of Wormsley and became a life long benefactor of cricket.

Paul Jr.'s son, Mark, assisted by Ronald's son, Christopher, as well as others in this generation, continued the rebuilding effort. At Mark's direction the family banded together to save Ronald from bankruptcy and establish a series of business enterprises that offered a place for any member of the Getty family willing to make an effort. By the mid-1990s, the Gettys had begun to crawl away from the emotionally sterile soulless passion of J. Paul Getty.

I have indicated that my grandfather was a classic example of this breed of unbalanced business leader. In his later years, he had little time for anything but work—he attended no religious services, engaged in no athletic pursuits, involved himself in no social organizations or community service. His social calendar was absorbed with company dinners and parties. As a result, while his passing was certainly mourned by those close to him, including countless people who worked at the company he founded, the company and family were left with a number of problems. Had he lived a more balanced, well-rounded life, he might have been able to foresee and manage these problems.

My grandfather, for instance, didn't take family vacations. Although he had some friends, he didn't have a large circle of friends. As those friends aged, he quickly ran out of surviving companions with whom to do things. Toward the end of his life, before he died at age 74, he suffered a partial stroke. It did not impact him in terrible ways except to curtail his ability to enjoy his already narrow spectrum of activities.

People who strive for a more balanced life generally have a wider range of interests and a larger circle of friends to enjoy these interests with than my grandfather. In his case, after the stroke, a company employee would fly to Dallas and drive him around the country for a few weeks at a time. I was sad. It was as if we had to manufacture a companion for him. This story is just another illustration of why balance in one's life is important.

Such outcomes are merely symptoms of the underlying problem, which is that some leaders have lived lives that are seriously out of balance. By focusing on business to the exclusion of almost every other aspect of life, they have created a lopsided existence, an out-of-kilter system that will likely not survive their absence. It may fall apart even while they work as hard as they can to keep it going.

I do not mean to criticize hard work—far from it. Nothing is wrong with hard work. Freud said happiness is love and work and, while much of what the Vienna doctor said has fallen into disrepute, I have seen nothing in my life to contradict this statement. The problem is over-attention to business—or over-attention to anything, for that matter. When any business leader devotes all his attention to a single topic, even one as important as the business, he creates a recipe for an unstable enterprise.

WHY BALANCE MATTERS

Try this. Stand on one foot and, without letting the other foot touch the ground, try to walk across the room and get a book. Obviously, hopping on one foot doesn't work as well as using both feet.

Now try this. Work all the time, 24/7, and devote none of your energies to your family, personal needs, or other aspects of life. This doesn't work very well either, but because many believe this lifestyle is necessary, even desirable, its impact is not as obvious as the walking example.

In the United States, professional effort is revered. We hear stories of doctors operating for 16 hours at a stretch, of factory workers pulling double shifts to get out a shipment on time, of negotiators talking all night to close a deal. We nod our heads and try to match these driven individuals in their single-minded pursuit of success at work.

But life is not one-dimensional. In fact, it's not two-dimensional or even three-dimensional. Life is multidimensional, with an endless array of possible arenas to exert your energy and attention. Can you choose too many areas? Of course. John Perry Barlow, lyricist for the musical group the Grateful Dead, once penned the line, "Too much of everything is just enough." Older and wiser now, he counters his earlier attitude with, "How thin can I spread myself before I'm no longer there?" You don't have to be a fan of rock music to appreciate the question.

In addition to being multidimensional, life is also an everchanging system. It's organic in the sense that its organization resembles that of a living organism, all parts interconnected and influencing one another. Your relations with your spouse, for instance, affect your relations with your coworkers, just as your physical health affects your ability to put in hours at the job. Ignoring one of these interconnected components in favor of concentrating solely on one is as risky as a sailor paying attention to only one line on a sailboat.

Further complicating the issue of balance in our lives is the fact that our lives are constantly changing. Each of us will experience normal life changes that will affect different dimensions. For example, family life to a 22-year-old just out of college and working at her first job may not be as important to her as when she is older, married, and caring for her first child. As we proceed through life, each of us will experience changes, and our balance of interests will likely shift.

Not all of the changes will be enjoyable or for the better. For instance, many of us will go through what is commonly known as a midlife crisis. As parents, many will suffer the empty-nest syndrome after the children mature and leave home. If we are CEOs, the day of our exit will arrive. Each of these normal changes can be a big deal or a not-so-big deal depending upon preparation. The extent to which you have developed a sense of balance prior to major transition events will in large part determine how significant change will impact you, your family, and your business.

WHAT IS A BALANCED LIFE?

Living a balanced life is a matter of merging one's many selves in a manner that is mutually supportive or, at the very least, mutually accommodating. This does not mean, by the way, that you devote precisely equal amounts of time, energy, and attention to everything. Nor does it mean that you should devise a schedule or a budget of attention and energy, divided by topic, and adhere rigidly to it. Balance in this sense is much like balance in the physical sense. You have to adjust frequently to bumps and changes, and you have to come up with your own definition of balance.

ACTION ITEM 4

The first step to achieve balance is to identify the areas of your life that you want to include. Only you can identify those in detail.

For one person, it may be impossible to live a balanced life without attending at least 15 major league baseball games per season. For another, keeping Saturday mornings free for painting landscapes could be just as vital a component of balance. From my experience, a balanced life has six primary areas: business, family, health, spiritual, social, and the self.

Business

Some view work as a calling. Because work is the way security and wealth are achieved, for some it can appear to be the mother of all necessities. I have found no magic number for the proper amount of time to devote to business. Forty hours a week may be a reasonable number for some people; 60 hours or 30 hours may be right for others.

One way to balance your business life is to put limits on the amount of time regularly devoted to specific business activities. Use a schedule. One successful business executive I work with starts his workday at 7 AM and quits at 6 PM five days a week. That's 55 hours a week, a heavier work schedule than most, yet it works for him. He doesn't work on weekends and, as a rule, doesn't work past 6 PM. This schedule allows him to balance the other areas of his life with business.

Family

Family life is usually central to anyone, whether they are involved in a closely held business or not. However, family life is often neglected in favor of business responsibilities. To balance, many families use the same strategy as for balancing business involvement. That is, instead of saying they will devote X hours per week to family pursuits, they simply set parameters. For instance, one business executive makes it a rule never to miss a significant event in his children's lives. Soccer games, dance recitals, school plays, and birthdays take precedence over business or other needs. This rule allows him considerable flexibility in pursuing other goals while ensuring a measure of balance when it comes to his family involvement.

Warning: taking your spouse and children to countless business functions doesn't count as pure family time for purposes of maintaining balance. That's not to advise against exposing your children to your work environment, something I recommend; just don't overload. Time spent around work is not family time simply because you are being accompanied by family members. Your head will still be business saturated, your presence only physical.

ACTION ITEM 5

Use the same strategy for balancing business involvement and family involvement. Set parameters. Make specific efforts to remain involved in your business; commit to balancing family involvement with other spheres of life.

Health

The personal health of closely held business leaders is of great importance, because they are the primary stewards and sources of security and prosperity. Excessive consumption of alcohol, chronic overeating, failing to exercise, or avoiding regular medical check-ups are all signs that business people have let the health aspect of their lives get out of balance. In contrast, the most successful leaders treat themselves as valuable assets to the business. They engage in routine physical maintenance and upkeep for themselves and avoid self-destructive personal practices, just as they do in caring for valuable facilities and equipment.

The Cooper Clinic is a world-renowned preventive healthcare facility created by Dr. Kenneth Cooper, a physician, who made aerobics a household name by penning the best-seller, *Aerobics*. The Cooper Clinic's 30-acre site is packed with jogging trails, treadmills, pools, weight circuits, and many other state-of-the-art exercise facilities. It's no vacation to spend time there, but a number of executives I know book Cooper Clinic appointments years in advance for the ultimate physical maintenance: a thorough medical examination, guidance in healthy eating and exercise, and time on the fitness gear. Many of my clients have been doing this every year for 20 or more years.

ACTION ITEM 6

Care for your health as you would any other valuable business asset. See that other leaders do the same with the valuable personal assets they bring to the business.

Spiritual

A prophet is not automatically a successful businessperson. I have dealt with successful business leaders who were deeply religious and those who have never set foot in a place of worship, nor apparently considered spiritual conundrums. However, even completely secular, pragmatic, successful business people recognize that they have spiritual needs that must be met. Accordingly, they at least provide their families and employees with the opportunity to attend religious services and to observe holy days. Again, as in the case of balancing business pursuits, it's a matter of setting reasonable parameters within which balance can exist.

Having a solid spiritual component helps leaders maintain respect and humility. It keeps us in touch with something larger than ourselves. It's not about going to a church or temple or any other house of worship, in small groups or large assemblies, and it's not an artificial construct so that people will one day attend your funeral. It is simply important that we have a presence in our life that keeps us in touch with causes that are greater than our own.

ACTION ITEM 7

Realize that many, if not most, of the people in your organization are likely to have spiritual needs, including yourself. Plan to provide these people with adequate opportunity to observe religious rites or otherwise address their metaphysical side.

Social

A balanced life requires that you have friends and make contributions to your community in one way or another. Life is not meant to be purely family or business or even just the two. Do successful businesspeople need friends? Are there business reasons for having a social life? Indeed there are.

When you get ready to retire, you have to have friends. They make retirement easier. It is easier for you to pass your business on to the next leader. It's possible for you to take a vacation. If you have no interests outside work, you will find it very difficult to let go of the one thing in your life that has meaning. As a paradoxical result, your failure to let go may doom the enterprise you have devoted your life to running. So make friends, get involved, and find out about life outside work. It could be the best thing you ever do for your company.

ACTION ITEM 8

Have friends. Make contributions to your community in one way or another. Being a social animal makes you a more effective leader.

Self

A balanced life means that you are also taking time for yourself. Call it selfish if you like, but if you don't respect and take care of yourself, you will find it difficult to respect and take care of others. You will be a less effective leader to the extent you fail in those duties.

Take time to read a book. Get a massage. Take a nap. Work in the garden. You need unallocated time to do nothing, free not only from work but also from time robbers. Taking care of you means giving yourself time to recover from work. Other people call this potting or replanting time. Make sure you're not one of those leaders who never take a day off to recover.

Taking care of the self is something of a grab bag. Some of the things you do for yourself may be spiritual, others social, and others to do with your health. The key is to be somewhat self-indulgent in addressing this need. I often use the metaphor of the flight attendant's instructions before every flight: "In the event of a loss of cabin pressure, oxygen masks will fall from the ceiling. If you are travelling with a child, place your mask on first and then secure another mask on the child." This makes the point cleanly: you must take care of yourself to take care of others.

ACTION ITEM 9

Take time to do things for yourself. You have to take care of yourself to take care of others.

Are these all the areas of life that a business leader must recognize? Not at all. Art, sports, hobbies, community service, and many other pursuits are conceivably parts of any business leader's plan for diversification. Balance is a fluid concept, one that must be felt as much as defined.

SYMPTOMS OF A BALANCED LIFE

You don't have to be in perfect balance all of the time, and everyone has periods in life when it is easy to be knocked off balance: divorce, death, illness, midlife crisis, empty nesting, time-sensitive projects (like writing a book), and periods when you have to work to rediscover yourself. That's normal. The difference between a balanced lifestyle and an unbalanced one is a coping system. The greatest risk a leader or executive who lives an unbalanced life can make is a decision in his own interest rather than in the interests of his stakeholders. Carried to an extreme, an out-of-balance life can manifest itself like an addiction, where the most important thing is satisfying the addiction, not taking care of the other aspects of your life. Such an extreme will produce detrimental consequences.

PORTRAIT OF SUCCESS

Jon Huntsman

Jon Huntsman managed to build one of the largest corporations in America while maintaining admirable balance in the other aspects of his life. Many business people have been as balanced, and a few as successful, but hardly anyone has been able to mingle the various components of a full life so well while achieving so much across the board.

Huntsman was born in Idaho in 1937 and was reared by parents of modest means. As a boy growing up in California, he picked produce, mowed lawns, and worked in a department store to earn money. An excellent student, he earned a college scholarship to the University of Pennsylvania, where he attended the Wharton School of Finance. After graduating with a master's degree from the University of Southern California, he entered the navy.

The seeds of his later business success were sown in the early 1960s, when Huntsman began working in the food distribution industry. He developed a plastic carton for holding eggs that worked better than the then-dominant paper cartons.

In 1969, he struck out on his own, forming Huntsman Container Corp. In a masterstroke, he convinced McDonald's to begin serving takeout hamburgers in a plastic clamshell container he had designed. Similar containers formed the basis of a product line sold to hospitals and many other users. In the 1980s, Huntsman got into chemicals and the production of a wide variety of plastics and resin products.

Huntsman's innovation, coupled with a savvy financial strategy of inexpensively buying companies going through cyclical downturns, helped him build Huntsman Corporation of Salt Lake City into the largest privately owned chemical company in the United States, with annual sales around $5 billion. The company employs nearly 10,000 people and is well regarded for its humanitarian and environmental practices.

Yet even these singular achievements nearly pale next to Huntsman's accomplishments in other areas of life. To begin with, he is a great philanthropist. Charitable giving has always been a part of his makeup, even early in his career when he was less than prosperous. As a billionaire, his gifts have continued.

He and his company contributed significantly to Armenian earthquake relief, building a concrete plant that has provided materials for new housing for 40,000 people whose homes were destroyed in the 1988 disaster. He and his corporation also teamed with international aid agencies to help distribute tens of thousands of cases of food and medical equipment to Armenia.

Huntsman has personally given more than $100 million to the University of Utah for cancer research. In addition, he raised another $51 million in donations to the same center from colleagues and business associates.

Charitable giving has not been the end of Huntsman's involvement in the public sphere. He was an assistant in the Nixon White House and later served as a United States Ambassador. Today, he and his wife sit on several hospital boards in Salt Lake City. No surprise that the arena where the National Basketball Association's Utah Jazz play is named The Jon M. Huntsman Center.

When it comes to his family life, Huntsman has been no less active and involved. He is the father of nine children, all of whom have been involved with the family business. In addition, his wife, Karen Huntsman, has served as vice president of the company since the beginning. The family is equally involved in the company. The entire family, even when the children were very young, met weekly to discuss the business and vote on decisions.

To go with everything else, Huntsman has a well-developed spiritual life. He and his wife are devout Mormons and have been active in the church all their lives. With all his accomplishments in personal, business, and civic spheres, Huntsman is truly the embodiment of the American dream. Fittingly, in 1997 he received the Horatio Alger Award recognizing distinguished Americans.

You may not be able to determine all the dimensions of your life or to precisely quantify how much effort and attention you should devote to each. But you can determine when your life is in balance by paying attention to some key indicators in the crucial matter of balancing work and other responsibilities.

One important indicator is the feeling that work is fulfilling. If you usually enjoy your work and look back on the day's accomplishments with pride and pleasure, you can be fairly certain that you are not overdoing it. If, on the other hand, you feel anxious and upset about work, even when you are devoting considerable attention to it and producing significant results, you may be out of balance. Just as the panicked, ineffective arm-waving of a tightrope artist warns of the coming fall, your discomfort and frenzied extra effort may presage a tumble of your own. So don't lose your passion, but don't lose your balance either. It may be a long way down, with no net to break the fall.

ACTION ITEMS

ACTION ITEM 1

Inculcating passion isn't enough. Any business must be financially successful to justify its own existence. It does no one any good to devote genius and inspiration to a commercial enterprise that is not commercially viable.

ACTION ITEM 2

Stressing what's best for employees and communities as well as owners can transform an enterprise from a business into a higher calling.

ACTION ITEM 3

Providing appropriate perks to those who have earned them will go a long way toward building a corporate culture that makes those working at the business believe they would never dream of working elsewhere.

ACTION ITEM 4

The first step to achieve balance is to identify the areas of your life that you want to include. Only you can identify those in detail.

ACTION ITEM 5

Use the same strategy for balancing business involvement and family involvement. Set parameters. Make specific efforts to remain involved in your business; commit to balancing family involvement with other spheres of life.

ACTION ITEM 6

Care for your health as you would any other valuable business asset. See that other leaders do the same with the valuable personal assets they bring to the business.

ACTION ITEM 7

Realize that many, if not most, of the people in your organization are likely to have spiritual needs, including yourself. Plan to provide these people with adequate opportunity to observe religious rites or otherwise address their metaphysical side.

ACTION ITEM 8

Have friends. Make contributions to your community in one way or another. Being a social animal makes you a more effective leader.

ACTION ITEM 9

Take time to do things for yourself. You have to take care of yourself to take care of others.

CHAPTER 7

Create Business Traditions, Myths, and Shared Beliefs

In the early days of Olan Mills, Inc., my grandfather's initial efforts to expand from his home base in Tuscaloosa, Alabama, into nearby Greenville, Alabama, nearly resulted in disaster. It starts off as a fairly typical tale of a start-up company trying to grow but severely constrained by a lack of capital. In a nutshell, he received such a poor reception that not one sale was made during the entire first week. The demoralized sales team, upon preparing to return to their home base in Tuscaloosa, found that the financially strapped founder had assured the rooming house owner of being paid by guaranteeing their personal belongings against the room and board account. So far so good. But what happened next made this story a piece of the corporate lore of Olan Mills, Inc. The founder exerted his legendary charm and persuasive powers to the maximum. He not only convinced the salespeople to try again, but he also inked the first sale—to that same rooming house's proprietor.

This story has been told time and again at Olan Mills, Inc. It could have been seen as an embarrassment to Olan Mills, but instead of being quashed, its retelling was encouraged. Why? Be-

stead of being quashed, its retelling was encouraged. Why? Because it carried with it a message that was an important part of the culture and attitude that made the company successful. It said that this was and had always been a company that wasn't afraid to take risks to pursue growth. It was a company where determination, resourcefulness, and salesmanship were highly valued. Moreover, it was a company that didn't give up just because it hit a rough patch. Olan Mills knew, as our ancient forebears did and as some modern business people are starting to rediscover, that traditions, myths, and shared beliefs are among the most powerful tools for turning individuals into cohesive, informed, coordinated teams and organizations.

PORTRAIT OF SUCCESS

Herbert Kelleher

The year was 1971, and two would-be airline executives, Herb Kelleher and Rollin King, were in a restaurant formulating their idea for a route system that would serve the major Texas cities. Kelleher took a cocktail napkin and sketched a triangle. He labeled one point of the triangle Dallas, one Houston, and one San Antonio. This was the foundation of the business model for Southwest Airlines, one of the most unlikely yet successful start-ups ever. It's also one of the most unlikely—and yet, they say, true—business stories around.

The sketch and the more detailed business plan the two entrepreneurs soon drew up helped them raise millions of dollars to launch their venture. They became a public company, expanding to other Texas cities and beyond. Today, Southwest Airlines is the fifth largest airline in America, taking off over 2,600 times a day and flying more than 57 million passengers a year to 60 cities coast to coast. Since achieving its first profitable year in 1973, Southwest has racked up 28 straight years in the black, recording $603 million in net income on revenues of $5.6 billion in 2000. Its sales were good enough for 316th place on the *Fortune* 500, and in 2001, it recorded not only the highest profit in the industry but was one of the few major airlines even to record a profit.

Lots of numbers here, but what stands out is the story. Not just because it's memorable, but also because it's been remembered. Southwest still remains the only major airline that specializes in short-haul, high frequency service. In other words, Kelleher's airline is still playing out the story line he drew up in 1971. Oh, and one more number. Southwest was ranked fourth on *Fortune's* list of best companies to work for. Does that tell you anything about a story's power to build corporate culture?

WHY BUSINESS TRADITIONS, MYTHS, AND SHARED BELIEFS MATTER

Truth: At the very foundation of long-term success is a shared vision or belief of what the future should look like. Without a common vision or shared values, no organization can muscle through the inevitable conflicts. There may be room for disagreement about a lot of things in business, but whether the leadership and ownership share similar views on such matters as people, work, and money will, in large part, determine the organization's ability to achieve sustainable success.

What the values actually are matters less than that the values are similar. In other words, if the shareholders want the money after a profitable year and the managers need the cash for expansion capital, conflict will erupt and someone, or some group, will likely lose in the end. Belief and value conflicts are the primary source of incompatible relationships, both personal and professional.

Try this. Pick someone nearby and challenge him to an arm wrestling match. The object is to win as often as you can within one minute. Each time you win, you receive a dollar. The loser receives nothing. Now start.

If you chose someone of near equal strength, you both probably struggled a bit and someone emerged as a victor, and richer.

Now try the same game, but this time think about the values involved. Is it important to have a winner and a loser? Could both players win? If you both had similar values of achieving your greatest gain, then you each might push the other to victory, thereby moving without struggle and racking up more total dollars, split equally. A simple value lesson, but one that almost never fails to elicit an "ah ha."

ACTION ITEM 1

No entity will achieve long-term, sustainable success without shared beliefs and values among owners and managers.

Business stories, traditions, and myths are unmatched at making information memorable. One of the best-known business stories concerns the tale of a customer who came into a unit of the Nordstrom's department store chain demanding a refund. Nordstrom's was and is legendary for its customer service. The admonition "the customer is always right" is only a hint of how rabid its employees are about pleasing customers. But the problem was, this customer wanted a refund for some tires he had bought, and Nordstrom's didn't sell tires. The customer service representative accepted the tires, issued the refund, and although his or her name wasn't recorded, instantly and permanently entered the lore of Nordstrom's and of retailing in general.

Who could forget that story? Anyone who hears it knows Nordstrom's will stop at nothing—nothing—to please a customer. If you want to make your message to employees, customers, or anyone else memorable, package it in a story. You can do nothing more effective to construct a durable corporate culture and cement the identification of employees, customers, suppliers, and others with your company. At savvy companies, similar tales exemplifying corporate traits are often told to job applicants. The idea is to see if they get it. If they do, odds are they will make a good fit. If they don't, odds are they won't, and they know it. When widely enough disseminated, corporate stories can even work to attract people who identify with them. For instance, the stories about the social activism and lifestyle of the founders of The Body Shop and Ben & Jerry's Ice Cream serve to encourage like-minded people to apply to work there, which creates a virtuous circle of reinforcing behavior with stories about behavior.

Imparting corporate values through stories also gives an unmatched ability to handle complex, ambiguous, and even contradictory messages. The perfect example is Aesop. This ancient Greek's simple fables of foxes, asses, and dogs break complex moral dilemmas into simple, easily understood, and remembered tales. Is there any better way to express how people sometimes pretend to reject the unattainable than the fable of the "Fox and the (Sour) Grapes"? If so, I haven't heard it.

Traditional stories are also wonderful for handling ambiguity, ambivalence, and other slippery concepts. For instance, many, if not most, companies are dogged by the contradiction between declaring, "Our people are our best assets," while also asserting, "The customer is king." How can you reconcile this? You could try to draw a line and say, for instance, any time a customer utters three offensive remarks in less than five minutes, the employee is allowed to calmly tell the customer to take a flying leap. But who can remember such a guideline when it's needed? Better to relate a dramatic account of an employee who experienced an abusive client and was backed up by superiors for asserting her rights.

PORTRAIT OF SUCCESS

Teresa Lever-Pollary

When things started going wrong for Teresa Lever-Pollary, she started collecting stories. The CEO of Nightime Pediatric Clinics, Inc., a 70-person company in Midvale, Utah, Lever-Pollary felt her company was losing touch with the values that had built it into one of the country's most successful after-hours, children's medical care providers.

So she started talking to patients and current and former employees, asking them to relate any stories they knew about the company. One was a nurse's anecdote of a doctor removing an ant from a child's ear by luring it out with a glob of cake frosting. Lever-Pollary felt the story of the MD's painless, innovative approach—especially the way he released the ant outdoors when it was over—highlighted the values she wanted to inculcate: gently but professionally caring for small living things.

Lever-Pollary didn't stop there. She gathered scores of stories and turned them into a book that is distributed to employees, suppliers, customers, job applicants, and others. Today, the book of Nightime Pediatrics stories serves the company as policy manual, training textbook, orientation course, values declaration, mission statement, and storehouse of corporate tradition and culture.

It's far more powerful than any manual or statement, Lever-Pollary realized one night. A veteran employee called the CEO at home. On the verge of tears, the nurse related how, for the first time ever, the storytelling exercise had shown her clearly how she contributed to the organization. That is the power of story.

Myths and stories define the culture of a company. In the absence of such myths, one can legitimately question whether you even have a company. Think about it. Virtually every business that is born from an entrepreneur's vision has a story to be told. There is the story of Alexander Graham Bell calling out, "Come here, Watson. I need you!" in the very first telephone call and setting in motion a company that, almost a century later, still marketed itself as a way to "reach out and touch someone." There is Michael Dell, selling computers direct from his college dorm room—a vivid reminder of Dell Computer's essential business model.

Now consider the many Internet start-ups created by venture capitalists in high-tech incubators. The management teams were assembled by people looking for a quick start-up, rapid growth, and a fast and rich cash-out. Where's the story there? "Let's round up some talented guys, and we'll run it?" The resounding crashes of so many soul-less, story-less, dotcom start-ups may be due as much to their lack of any real anecdote of beginning as to their lack of a market.

Stories can have negative effects, too. Where you have a history of bad management decisions, stories may be told that build them into the culture of your company. The founder of a Southeastern industrial service company is a highly emphatic person who combines a dogmatic attitude with a grease-under-the-fingernails aura of physicality. In practical terms, that means he reads people the riot act, getting nose to nose and, not uncommonly, threatening to resort to fisticuffs. On one occasion, I listened to the founder berate a man 40 years younger, screaming and threatening to take it outside. Events like these can't help but be retold and become part of corporate lore. Not surprisingly, a year or so later, I noticed two managers at the company were beginning to handle their own differences this way. Bad stories that get passed down can have a negative impact if no changes have occurred.

THE STORY OF STORIES

Almost all great leaders, business and otherwise, are also great storytellers. From the folksiness of Warren Buffett to the Hollywood polish of Ronald Reagan, people who can motivate others often do so through the medium of stories. It's always been that way, from the gentle parables of Jesus to the even earlier Chinese folk tales passed down by Confucius. Since those early, even prehistoric times, we have gone further and further toward explicit instructions, consisting of lists of policies and crossreferenced guidelines. Those approaches are challenged by the complexity of life today, as we may be reaching the limits of policy. We learn in multiple ways, but one of the most effective ways is through stories. How you pass cultures down in a business is through stories. You don't learn math by stories, but you learn history through stories. I impart business lessons by telling lots of stories. Why? Often, I find that people can't see their own errors when I point them out. However, if I tell them a parallel story about someone else (nameless, of course) who made the same mistake, the misstep is easier for them to absorb.

Stories, too, tap deep levels of humanity. They do more than transmit information; they create faith. They also allow us to change behavior at a much deeper and more lasting level than simply passing out instructions can accomplish. To change actions, change feelings. To change feelings, tell stories.

How to Do It

Creating corporate myths starts with understanding what makes a good story. That varies, of course, in the details, but generally a good story is brief, true, and specific. You should be able to tell your story whether you are launching into a lunchtime speech, having a brief conference around the water cooler, or writing it in the company newsletter.

To be really effective, a story should also be true. That's not always an ironclad requirement. For instance, the 6666 Ranch is a huge Texas ranching operation that traces its roots from the 1870s. The tale is still told of how the founder, Samuel Burk Burnett, won the stake that allowed him to set up as a rancher in a poker game. His winning hand, according to the legend, was four sixes. Actually, historians believe Burnett more likely saved earnings from his work as a trail boss to purchase his first herd. The fact is, the Four Sixes doesn't have to rely on fables for its fame. Among other things, it was chosen as a location for several Marlboro cigarette television commercials and also has served as a setting for Western movies. But the winning poker hand makes a great story and un-questionably contributes to the organization's culture and mys-tique, so it's persisted.

Specificity brings a story to life and encourages listeners to view it as relevant. Providing specific times, dates, and places increases the influencing potential of a story and helps people visualize what you're talking about. It's often important to describe pre-cisely what happened. Just saying, "And so the account executive handled the customer complaint and everyone lived happily ever after . . . ," isn't nearly as effective as describing how the account executive actually burst into tears in sympathy with the customer before collecting herself and handing over a certificate good for a free product worth more than the object of complaint.

When it comes to names, you should include them whenever possible. Sometimes confidentiality and good taste will keep you from attaching a name to an embarrassing misstep. But when you can, give the name of the just-hired worker who saved the day or the supplier who joined in like a comrade to get a rush order out the door. People relate best to other people, and the more actual, named people in your stories, the more personal and effective they will be.

Gathering Your Corporate Stories

So where are you going to get all these stories? Answer: If you want to get stories that influence people, go to the people themselves. Ask your employees to relate tales to you. Lever-Pollary polled her employees systematically, hiring a consultant to aid in the process. She also talked to ex-employees and patients while using a tape recorder to capture their stories about the company. Once transcribed, the stories were edited and shown to their original tellers to confirm the details.

ACTION ITEM 2

To get stories that influence people, go to the people. Interview employees, ex-employees, customers, and others, asking them to tell you any stories about your company.

Disseminating corporate stories can be done through the company newsletter, postings on bulletin boards, and even printed paycheck inserts. But the most effective way to disseminate stories is face to face. Sales meetings, annual meetings, quarterly meetings, departmental meetings, even casual chats in the hallway—all are opportunities to marry the power of corporate storytelling with the influence of face-to-face communication.

ACTION ITEM 3

The most effective way to disseminate stories is face to face. Prepare stories for sales meetings, annual meetings, quarterly meetings, departmental meetings, and casual hallway chats, and insert them into your corporate culture the way a physician injects a vaccine.

CREATING TRADITIONS

Like it or not, we all rely on traditions to one degree or another. The important thing to remember about traditions is that because we will all have them, we can choose either to plan and create them or let someone else create them for us by default. Traditions foster group identity and can serve as a glue to bring people together. Within family held businesses, traditions assume an added benefit of keeping shareholders aware of the family business heritage. But, before you start creating and spreading your business traditions and stories, you will want to select among those available to you. The stories you want are the ones that will make a good tradition through strengthening the corporate culture, helping others identify with the company, and advancing specific corporate values. For instance, Feargal Quinn, the Irish supermarket magnate I mentioned previously, relates this story about his company's beginning.

Before World War II, Feargal's father and uncle worked together in the family business, also a grocery, until one day they found themselves at odds and decided they could no longer work together. They agreed one of them would buy the other's interest in the company and decided to use a coin toss to decide how to value it. The winner of the toss would set the price and would offer it for sale to the other, who would either buy it or receive that amount of money for his share.

Feargal's father won the toss and set the price so high that he was sure his brother would never pay it. His brother, however, accepted the price and paid the money, and that's how Feargal's father was forced out of the family business. That's not the end of the story. With money from the sale, he went into the grocery business on his own and created the company that provided Feargal with his first exposure to the grocery industry. The story emphasizes Quinn's lengthy history in the industry and stresses that you have to always see things from the customer's viewpoint unless you want a possibly unpleasant surprise.

In retail businesses, including grocery stores and photography studios, the holiday buying season is critical to revenues and profitability. In the mid-70s, Olan Mills, Inc., introduced a new product, the Deluxe Canvas portrait. Never had we produced something as large or as expensive. It was perfect for display over the fireplace in an elegant home, in corporate boardrooms honoring past leadership, or other similar settings of great honor.

This top-of-the-line product had to be handmade and, unfortunately, we discovered that we had grossly underestimated the amount of time required to ship a product that satisfied our standards. At the same time, we were discovering production problems, our troops in Denver, Colorado, decided to lower the price and promote this new product aggressively with contests and special incentives for employees—at the height of the Christmas season rush.

To further complicate the situation, the aggressive sales team sold on the belief that the customers would receive their Deluxe Canvas portrait prior to December 25th. Not surprisingly, the Denver team sold tremendously more than any other sales team in the company. It appeared inevitable that we would miss the deadline in Denver.

What happened next? The president of Olan Mills, Inc., loaded up the corporate jet with portraits promised for Christmas and flew the jet from Tennessee to Denver. The pilots were met at the airport by local management who unloaded the plane and personally drove to customers's homes, delivering the portraits as promised in time for the holiday.

The moral of that story was that we would stick to our promises and when we charge customers for premium products, we do what's necessary to make them right. This has become a significant bit of corporate lore at Olan Mills, Inc., with positive consequences.

ACTION ITEM 4

Pick corporate stories that will make a positive tradition, strengthen corporate culture, identify with the group, and specify corporate values.

Note that not all corporate stories have to have happy endings. The tale of how your employees worked hard one holiday weekend packing and express shipping a large, unexpected rush order, only to have the customer declare bankruptcy the following week, can illustrate positive values while not being a happy story. In this case, the value would be in the company's insistence on performing adequate credit checks and only selling to customers who can pay.

Spotting Your Own Traditions

The best place to find stories about the past is to go to the past. To scavenge anecdotes about your company's traditions, talk to veteran employees, ex-employees, and long-time customers, and perhaps best of all, company retirees. Don't neglect printed sources either. Articles published about your company, old company newsletters, corporate histories, minutes from company meetings, reports, memos, and letters can all provide grist for the story mill.

ACTION ITEM 5

Traditions may need to be consciously maintained at first until, through the passage of time, they take on a life of their own. Rather than just telling them once, repeat selected traditions at appropriate opportunities.

You can inject tradition-building stories into your company the same way you do any story. However, maintaining traditions is especially important, because only through the passage of time do they take on a life of their own. So rather than just telling them once, take selected traditions and repeat them.

Around every Christmas, for example, you can have a set of stories relating to the way the company employees work hard and as a supportive team to deal with the holiday rush. Not all traditions have to be stories, by the way. A tradition, such as reverence for the customer, can be celebrated by giving the employee who achieves the highest monthly customer service rating the best parking spot, right by the front door. Even better, hold a ceremony on the first of each month in which the sign marking the spot as the possession of last month's winner is taken down and a new one is installed. A tradition honoring innovation can be maintained by keeping a museum full of devices and designs on which your company has received patents, similar to the way a tribal medicine doctor might keep a hut full of totems purporting to contain magical power. Silly? Perhaps, but we are people, and we relate well to such rituals and symbols.

It's critical that people who are new to your organization, whether customers, employees, or suppliers, be exposed to your traditional corporate stories. When you are just starting a relationship, you know little about each other and are understandably nervous and reluctant to commit. Telling stories about your company as a way to start a fresh association is a good way to overcome that reluctance and turn strangers into team members.

BUILDING SHARED BELIEFS

When you believe one thing and I believe another, we're not positioned for a productive relationship as team members. In business, teamwork starts with having some sense of shared belief, some common vision of what the future is going to look like. That is the foundation for growth. If we don't share a common belief and vision, growth won't happen.

When Hewlett-Packard's CEO, Carly Fiorina, led the charge to acquire Compaq in 2001, she met with unanticipated dissent over the vision and leadership beliefs of cofounders William Hewlett and David Packard. In the CEO's mind, the acquisition meant a merging of powerful name brands and complementary products. To the children of the cofounders, it meant laying off possibly 15,000 HP employees. Quoted in the *New York Times,* son David Packard stated, "Bill and Dave never developed a premeditated business strategy that treated HP employees as expendable." Meanwhile a daughter, Susan Packard Orr, announced, "HP does not exist to make a profit; it exists to make a contribution." A conflict of beliefs has cost this company hundreds of millions of dollars.

Shared beliefs themselves are the end result of sharing stories and company traditions. Stories, rituals, awards, and totems affect belief rather than just providing information. But building shared beliefs involves more than just employing these tools. You have to pick the right source of beliefs, direct them to the right people, and be sure they are consistent with the company's actual behavior if you want them to work.

To build shared beliefs, start with shared experience. For employees, on-the-job experiences are obviously key. It is questionable whether relating stories about behavior away from work can do much to build shared beliefs at work.

Don't neglect to celebrate the importance of people who are not high on the organization chart. Make a special effort to identify and disseminate stories and build and maintain traditions that emphasize the value of everyone in your company, but especially those on the lowest rungs. It's fine to distribute a memo announcing that a team led by the new vice president of sales has closed a major account. But, when an administrative assistant with 20 years on the job invents a new filing system that saves time and reduces space, then you are missing a great opportunity if you fail to harvest and sow this story.

ACTION ITEM 6

Celebrate people who are not high on the organization chart. Make a special effort to identify and disseminate stories and build and maintain traditions that emphasize the value of everyone in your company, but especially those on the lowest rungs.

Your stories and traditions have to be consistent and clear to work to the utmost. One way to help this come about is to include the moral of the story any time you relate it. If you don't provide the moral, someone may draw the wrong conclusion from your story. Follow Aesop's example and explicitly state the point of your story if it could be construed as promoting beliefs, traditions, or behaviors you don't want.

ACTION ITEM 7

Include the moral of any story you relate. Otherwise, someone might draw exactly the wrong conclusion from your story, and it could have the opposite effect from what you intended.

Finally, you must exemplify these beliefs and values. Telling stories won't overcome reality. People will place more credence in what they see you do than they will in a legend about something you used to do, or might have done once.

ACTION ITEM 8

You must exemplify by your actions the beliefs and values you want to build. Telling stories won't overcome reality.

One particular event, which became a story for me to tell, still stands solidly after 23 years. One of the greatest fallacies of effective leadership is the notion that the leader should always know what to do and have all the answers. Many people believe this, but it is simply not accurate. To convince others to rid themselves of this fallacy, I demonstrate my vulnerability by telling the story of when I was afraid that I had "overheated" my responsibilities and feared driving the business into a tailspin.

As a newly promoted district manager, I was assigned a territory widely regarded as the company's worst. It ranked last in almost every performance category. It was also staffed by many people who had a lot more years than I in the company. When I began to make sweeping changes in the way everybody did their work, I may have overdone it somewhat. That's excusable, I believe. After all, we had just come off a year with 700 percent turnover—not a time for tinkering. I closed stores, fired people, and took all the actions involved in a turnaround. I was 25 and had not experienced much. I was going on what I thought was right.

I vividly remember the phone call late on a Friday night during which I began to doubt my wisdom. One of my senior managers had decided to quit, and I immediately feared others would follow. Although I desperately needed this person at that moment to fill a slot, the employee had decided to leave, and I knew I had no choice but to accept the resignation. But I did wonder: Someone who'd been with the company 15 years was walking out on my watch. I remember in that moment thinking, "Do I put up a façade that I'm not affected by this and just press on, or do I ask for help?"

I thought about my dilemma for a few days. I was very afraid that the entire project I was working on would fall apart, that I had gone too far and moved too fast in making changes. Fearing my colossal mistakes might ruin the company, let alone my career, on impulse I called my boss and told him the entire story, including what my fears were. He just listened while I talked. Yet with no counsel or advice from him, I was able to gain an important perspective. The greatest lesson I learned was that I have to talk to other people who aren't so wrapped up in events and don't have their egos attached to them. I learned a truly valuable insight.

That small lesson was huge for me. Although the manager did quit, his leaving turned out to be no big deal. Meanwhile, the moral: I learned that it was okay to talk about fears and shortcomings as a leader.

THE DOWNSIDE

Stories aren't like numbers in a spreadsheet. They can add up differently for different people. That's why you have to pick carefully the stories you want to spread and provide the moral you want listeners to take away. Once the wrong story or the wrong interpretation gets out, you may have a lot of trouble stamping it out or replacing it with a better one.

Managing by "storying around," as this leadership technique has been called, also has distinct limitations. For instance, if you do a really good job of building group identification, you may create a bunch of people who are so insular and inward looking that they become hostile to people and ideas from outside the organization. This sort of "not invented here" attitude rejecting all external influences has been responsible for the decline and fall of many once glorious enterprises.

Another risk is that you may, in your work at building traditions, cause your organization to glory in its brilliant past to the extent that it becomes blind to the future. You don't want to become too backward looking, or you will find it impossible to steer the organization toward a future of sustained success. So keep your story-building efforts looking forward, and keep an open mind to the powerful possibilities of a good story. Next time you're in a restaurant and your table server hands you a cocktail napkin, ask yourself, "What story could I tell on the back of this napkin, or involving this napkin, that could create a company that, 30 years later, would be worth billions of dollars?" It worked for Herb Kelleher, or at least that's the story.

ACTION ITEMS

ACTION ITEM 1

No entity will achieve long-term, sustainable success without shared beliefs and values among owners and managers.

ACTION ITEM 2

To get stories that influence people, go to the people. Interview employees, ex-employees, customers, and others, asking them to tell you any stories about your company.

ACTION ITEM 3

The most effective way to disseminate stories is face to face. Prepare stories for sales meetings, annual meetings, quarterly meetings, departmental meetings, and casual hallway chats, and insert them into your corporate culture the way a physician injects a vaccine.

ACTION ITEM 4

Pick corporate stories that will make a positive tradition, strengthen corporate culture, identify with the group, and specify corporate values you hold.

ACTION ITEM 5

Traditions may need to be consciously maintained at first until, through the passage of time, they take on a life of their own. Rather than just telling them once, repeat selected traditions at appropriate opportunities.

ACTION ITEM 6

Celebrate people who are not high on the organization chart. Make a special effort to identify and disseminate stories and build and maintain traditions that emphasize the value of everyone in your company, but especially those on the lowest rungs.

ACTION ITEM 7

Include the moral of any story you relate. Otherwise, someone might draw exactly the wrong conclusion from your story, and it could have the opposite effect from what you intended.

ACTION ITEM 8

You must exemplify by your actions the beliefs and values you want to build. Telling stories won't overcome reality.

CHAPTER 8

Do the Strongest Really Survive?

Q: How big do you have to be to survive anything the business world can throw at you?

A: This is a trick question. While being big can be an advantage, sheer size has little to do with the ability to survive over long periods and experience sustainable business success.

If you find that proposition unlikely, consider the companies that were once number one in their fields—truly vast enterprises that loomed over entire industries and even whole economies—yet now are no more. There is Pullman, once synonymous with railroad sleeper cars and as well known as Xerox is today. Pan American was once the world's largest airline but today survives only in memory. Montgomery Ward, although it never surpassed its rival Sears & Roebuck, was in position to challenge Sears at the end of World War II, but it was driven into bankruptcy in 1997 and disappeared. More recently, Enron, at a $65 billion dollar market capitalization, became the largest ever business bankruptcy.

PORTRAIT OF SUCCESS

Stora Enso

One of the world's oldest enterprises began in 1288, when the king of Sweden signed a charter granting mining rights to Kopparberg Mountain. Today, that organization survives as Stora Enso Oyj, the world's second-largest forest products concern, based in Helsinki and with annual sales exceeding $12 billion.

Just looking at the bare facts of Stora raises a couple of questions. How does a company survive more than 700 years? And how do you go from copper mining to paper mills?

The answer to both questions, as it turns out, is: Adaptability. Stora has a centuries-old tradition of exploiting natural resources in a sustainable manner and of modifying its techniques and even its basic businesses to fit the realities of current markets, technologies, and opportunities. The willingness and ability to do whatever it takes to survive have allowed it to stick around and prosper past its seventh centennial.

Stora's ancestral predecessor, the mining company, experienced many upheavals during its first few centuries of operation. Improved mining techniques were imported from Germany and led to major increases in production in the 17th century. All that came down with a literal crash in 1650 in a massive collapse at the mine. By 1750, however, the company had begun to process slag by-products from copper smelting to produce sulfuric acid and, as a by-product, a commodity called Falun Red Paint that would become its signature product, traditionally used in Sweden to paint wooden houses.

Paint carried Stora for more than 100 years, after which it purchased one of the world's largest sawmills, becoming heavily involved in pulp and chemicals about the same time. In 1900, it began manufacturing paper, establishing a newsprint mill and over the years developing new techniques for bleaching paper pulp. The company eased out of mining and metal processing. By its 700th anniversary in 1988, Stora was one of the largest forest products concerns in Europe. A few years later, it shut down the historic Falun Mine and Works.

The twists and turns of Stora's elongated history illustrate the necessity and the benefit of being able to evolve effectively. Though Stora is one of the world's biggest at what it does now, it wasn't always that way. The company's ability to change and adapt has served it well in maintaining and building upon seven centuries of success.

What are companies that survive devoted to if not to being the biggest? It turns out that long-term development, adaptability, learning, and evolution are all more important that mere size when it comes to building shareholder wealth over an extended time. We're all familiar with the concept of survival of the fittest. Given that the fittest survive, the question is: what is fitness for survival? It's not mere size—or strength, wealth, market share, longevity, reputation, etc. It's adaptability.

Companies that last a long time do typically grow larger in size. But they don't grow in an uncontrolled manner with expansion and mass as the only goals. Rather, they add on skills, new markets, and capabilities almost as living things do. At the same time, they may cut and prune unneeded or unhealthy parts as they go. The end result is an organization that, while it may not be and never will be the biggest, adapts to change and is positioned for long-term prosperity.

ACTION ITEM 1

Focus on being the most adaptable business, not the biggest.

WHY WE DON'T CHANGE

The idea that change is important is neither new nor obscure. It's widely known and appreciated that we live in an era where the rate of change is faster than ever, and not only continuing, but even accelerating. Why, then, do people and organizations fail to change?

One important reason is that some changes seem too large, too difficult, and too overwhelming. Even minor change, something as simple as taking a different route to work, can, in the presence of embedded habit, seem so uncomfortable that we will avoid it. Confronted with tasks we deem impossible or too uncomfortable, we do the sensible thing (under the circumstances) and hide our heads in the sand. The problem with this approach is that it is unrealistic on two counts. First, hiding our heads in the sand won't change the facts. Second, as a general rule, change looks harder than it is. That's understandable, because change by definition involves doing things differently than we are used to doing them.

When I encounter a situation where change is not occurring because the people in charge are feeling overwhelmed, I reframe the issue by presenting it as improving their skills to adapt. Rather than change the way they hire, for example, I teach them to do a second interview and check references. Looking at change as increasing adaptability rather than a criticism of what was being done knocks down barriers and eases the transition.

Another obstacle to change is the idea that responsibility for change belongs to someone else. This spin-off of the head-in-the-sand approach is, unfortunately, no more effective. The challenge of getting someone to believe that they—not someone else—must change is not a simple or easy one to master. Again, I try to approach this as an education or study project. We aim to explore change, not enforce it—at least not at first. As time goes by and the client becomes more accustomed to the idea of change and familiar with the advantages of adaptability, it begins to look like a better idea.

Countless antiquated business practices are followed simply because the people responsible don't think they have the time to change. This attitude has some validity. Change takes time, and we never seem to have enough time. Bob Lutz, the dynamic General Motors executive who took over the car giant's product design in 2001, is dealing with change obstacles in a big way. One of his toughest efforts is to get GM designers to move away from fulfilling internal design requirements and focus on giving customers attractive, desirable vehicles. The problem, of course, is that people at the world's biggest carmaker haven't had to change much, and they're not used to it.

One way to deal with this challenge is to clear off your desk and begin identifying needed changes, finding opportunities for building in adaptability and researching the resources necessary to implement them. As with most things, action precedes motivation—once you get started, you find you are committed and you find the time.

Fear is behind much reluctance to adapt. We may believe that it is too late to change or that we are too old to change. Sometimes, of course, this is the case. Many people are only motivated to change when failure is inevitable. But regret is no substitute for advance preparation. So we must forge ahead toward adaptability in spite of our misgivings. Observing other people who have changed at late dates in life can be comforting. For example, the former insurance agent Tom Clancy penned his first novel after age 40. Another way to defuse fear is to confront it. Trying small changes and looking for small improvements can give people a nonthreatening way to approach change.

Of course, effective change involves more than simply being willing to change. In an earlier chapter, I referenced the tale of TippingPoint, a company that was only too willing to change. For adaptability to be a powerful tool, it has to be paired with a solid, proven business model. The risk is that you don't move away from that proven model when times change. That's when adaptability becomes a paramount virtue. Take, for example, what General Electric did a few years ago when it decided to get out of the appliance business. A company with many decades' of experience in a field that decided, based on practical analysis, that it didn't need to be in that business any longer. A nonadaptable company might have kept competing with rivals in low-cost countries and self-destructed.

WHY PEOPLE AND ORGANIZATIONS DO CHANGE

Despite barriers to change, many people and organizations do successfully change, and many evince admirable levels of adaptability over long periods. Perhaps it is not to our credit as a species to say that the main reason people change is that they learn, or believe, that they simply must to survive. In other words, external forces propel us to change, as when a small business operating in a sheltered market suddenly finds itself subject to the full brunt of global competition. For instance, many local retailers unlocked their doors one day only to confront a sign across the street that said "Coming Soon—A Wal-Mart Superstore" or the like. These retailers are carried willy-nilly into rapid change—change that may be dominated unfortunately, by their going out of business.

Internal forces also motivate change. Biological or personal imperatives such as the desire to start a family, to build a legacy, to create a name, or simply to retire and rest may drive successful change efforts. Internal forces are often difficult to identify and tap—even when we are trying to identify our own internal forces. But if you can employ an internal force to bring about change, then you have overcome one of the major obstacles to successful change.

Yet another force is a combination of external and internal pressure. When others, especially people close to us, encourage us and support us to change, change can become much easier and more productive. That's why incorporating adaptability as a core value of a company whenever possible is important. When surrounded by people who understand the difficulty of change, appreciate the risks of failure accompanying change, and support the effort, change happens far more readily and consistently. Context is another very important reason for people being willing or unwilling to change. As I have noted in the remedies to change resistance cited above, change is much more likely to be embraced when presented as nonthreatening and safe.

STAGES OF CHANGE

Sometimes change happens very slowly, sometimes very quickly. The automobile industry has been going through a drawn out shakeout for the last 50 years, as the likes of Rambler and Jeep have disappeared into the maws of the Big Three and, most recently, one of the Big Three has consolidated into DaimlerChrysler. In machine tools, a far more sweeping shakeout took place during just a few years of the 1980s, when the majority of U.S. machine tool makers, amounting to hundreds of firms, disappeared in a very short time.

During these periods, the participants in these industries have been forced to change, accommodating new ideas about globalization, quality control, automation, technology, and customer service whether they wanted to or not. Whether change happens quickly or slowly, it usually moves through four stages: denial, anger, acceptance, and behavioral actions. If you can recognize which stage of change you are in currently, you will have an idea of how close you are to resolving the change issue.

Stage I: Denial

In this stage, change seems unnecessary or irrelevant. The person who needs to change either is unaware or seems to be unaware that change is imperative. At some level, however, the disturbing knowledge is beginning to creep in. The only obstacle to full awareness is a thin, eroding layer of denial.

Stage II: Anger

At stage II, the necessity for change has been accepted but the positive possibilities of change have not. The natural response to this perceived no-win situation is anger. People at this stage may rage; they may propose drastic but unfeasible ideas to render change unnecessary. What they don't do is calmly acknowledge and confront what must be done.

Stage III: Acceptance

By the third stage, both the necessity and acceptance for change have been internalized, and the individual is ready to assess what must be done. This is the first overtly positive stage in the change process, when distracting or destructive attitudes are replaced by evaluation, information gathering, and the germ of constructive activity.

Stage IV: Behavioral Actions

In the fourth stage, the behavioral actions that embody change have begun to take place. Sometimes, the behavioral modifications are done willingly and with full awareness. Other times, they seemingly take place without the person's knowledge or conscious effort.

OUT OF FOCUS

"Chainsaw" Al Dunlap

When Al Dunlap stepped into the job of chairman and chief executive officer at Scott Paper in 1994, investors cheered. Scott was seen as poorly managed at the time, and Dunlap, who had earned his sobriquet "Chainsaw Al" for his draconian cost-cutting efforts at other companies, was viewed as a savior.

Dunlap began doing what he was supposed to, firing thousands of employees and closing plants with energy. In just 18 months, he cut a deal to sell Scott to Kimberly-Clark for more than double the company's market valuation when he arrived. Once again, investors roared their approval, and Dunlap preened like a champion. Then the truth came out. Dunlap had cut far too much from research and development, plant maintenance, and other essentials in an effort to inflate the company's profits temporarily. Fixing the problems caused by Dunlap's unrestrained cost-cutting cost Kimberly-Clark hundreds of millions of dollars

This fact went unnoticed by large shareholders in Sunbeam, the leading U.S. manufacturer of small appliances such as toasters and coffeemakers, who decided Dunlap was just what that company needed. In 1996, Dunlap took over the chairman and CEO post at Sunbeam. Investors immediately began bidding up the stock, expecting another Scott Paper enrichment scheme.

But the real fruits of the Sunbeam episode were not profits, but truth. Dunlap was booted out just two years later, after doing so much damage to the venerable appliance concern that it wound up filing Chapter 11 bankruptcy. In the aftermath of the disaster, it was revealed that Dunlap, rather than being a skillful cost cutter, was often arbitrary in his decision making, dictatorial in the way he treated people, and fast and loose with the truth when it came to Sunbeam's accounting. Many cuts were made without regard for their long-term effect or whether they actually contributed to profitability. The way Dunlap treated the people at Sunbeam led to such hard feelings, that the executive reportedly purchased a gun and a bulletproof vest.

Among Dunlap's failings was the critical one of believing his own press releases. Shareholders lauded his abilities so much, that they allowed him not only to take the top job but stuff the board of directors so that he, in effect, could not be fired. In the end, of course, Dunlap was fired. Eventually, along with other Sunbeam executives, he paid $15 million to settle a lawsuit that charged him and others with fraudulently inflating the stock price. Now he's gone down in some people's eyes as one of the most amazing disappointments in American business history.

CEO-ITIS

One of my clients is a family-owned, East Coast business operating a professional services firm that has experienced rapid growth. Over the last five years, sales have grown from $20 million to more than $250 million. Yet, despite the apparent prosperity, the company is racked with conflict. I became involved when the CEO contacted me to help her find a buyer for the company. She wanted to sell because she found the meddling of other family members intolerable. I was able to find a buyer willing to pay nearly $100 million for a 50 percent share of the company. The CEO would be able to keep her job, and so would the other family member. This part of the deal was a key problem from the CEO's perspective, because it would not give her what she wanted, namely, the meddling family member to be completely out.

I presented the offer to the family owners, a group of four people. One half the group was in favor of the deal. The CEO and her spouse were opposed because the offer didn't remove the other family member from her job. In the end, the group was split, and the deal was not consummated. The company kept operating in its former state of conflict, with substantial resources of time, attention, and energy being siphoned off to deal with the angry CEO, the interfering family member, and negative emotions.

What happened here? As I see it, this was a clear case of CEO-itis. The CEO was out of touch with what was best for the company and its stakeholders and was thinking only of what she wanted. She cared more for the trappings of power, the big office and people jumping to her command, than she did the ability to create wealth in a sustainable fashion.

The symptoms of CEO-itis are consistent and fairly easy to spot. One of the most significant consists of a loss of perspective, as the executive becomes so inward looking that he is unwilling to look at problems from anyone else's viewpoint. When an executive makes moves that run counter to the advice he is receiving from people who are knowledgeable and reliable, that can be a sign of CEO-itis. If the leader offers no, or inadequate, reasons for disregarding outside counsel, it's another sign.

A CEO suffering from CEO-itis is also often overly concerned with getting and keeping power and the trappings of power. When a leader makes decisions that compromise the welfare of the company to boost her own prestige and influence, that's a strong indicator of CEO-itis.

Causes of CEO-itis

Where does CEO-itis come from? Unlike many of the exotic infectious diseases that concern humanity in the 21st century, such as the HIV and Ebola viruses, nobody is suggesting that CEO-itis comes from another animal. It's a purely human condition, one that we allow to grow in leaders through a set of distinct mistakes.

The first and foremost cause of CEO-itis is isolation. CEOs are overwhelmingly protected and often do not have the same access to information as underlings. Accurate and complete information is one of the main requirements for effective decision making. When a CEO is deprived of information, CEO-itis is likely to follow. CEOs are busy, to be sure, but they can't be too busy to be kept up on what is going on. If a CEO is not receiving the reports that would convey a grasp of the activities and status of the whole organization, the climate is ripe for an infestation of CEO-itis.

The information most likely kept from a CEO is bad news. It makes sense, of course, for employees to avoid bringing news about a sales shortfall, a lost customer, or a margin miscalculation. But that is precisely the type of information a CEO most needs to fend off an attack of CEO-itis. Candid reports of developments that aren't pleasing will bring a CEO's feet to earth, encourage careful consideration before acting, and forestall even an imminent case of CEO-itis.

ACTION ITEM 2

Make sure the CEO knows what's going on and, if necessary, document your information in writing to the CEO.

Passage of Time/Failure to Learn

Sometimes CEOs seem incapable of learning. As time passes, you see them making the same mistakes over and over.

As the rate of change accelerates and instability permeates even the calmest backwater of business, the ability to adapt to new situations is brought into strong focus. An executive who can't adapt to new situations will shortly be revealed as incompetent, as his ability to respond effectively to altering circumstances is outstripped by modifications in the environment.

This happened to Montgomery Wards in the period immediately after World War II. The head of the retailer was convinced that the postwar period would be one of massive unemployment and national depression, as the war industries laid off unnecessary workers and government payrolls shrunk. Instead, of course, the years after World War II were a time of bustling prosperity as pent-up consumer demand fueled rapid growth. But Montgomery Wards missed out on nearly all of this because the company's leader, Sewell Avery, refused to endorse any expansion. Rivals such as Sears built new stores at a rapid clip, adding capacity to service rapacious consumer demand. Avery sat and waited years for a depression that never came, stubbornly sticking to his theories even as time proved them wrong.

ACTION ITEM 3

When formerly successful tactics no longer produce the expected results, listen to those people closest to the action.

REMEDIES FOR CEO-ITIS

The most forthright way to deal with a case of CEO-itis is to get a new CEO. In fact, this treatment is often most beneficial, or the only, way to deal with the ailment. It may be nearly impossible to dismantle the systems, such as excessive pampering and perks and protection from unpleasant news, that have created an ailing CEO. One usually effective method, if time allows, is to revamp the board of directors to create a more candid environment. But many CEOs are people of strong personality, and getting a settled CEO to change her ways may be very difficult.

If all else fails, turnover at the top is one technique for coping with CEO-itis. It's also the best way to prevent it. A CEO who has been at the head of a company for, say, 25 or 30 years is almost certainly out of step, out of touch, and getting too comfortable with the prestige and power of the position. There are exceptions, to be sure. Jack Welch's quarter-century reign atop General Electric is one. But even Bill Gates turned over the CEO's title to his lieutenant, Steven Ballmer, approximately 25 years after Microsoft's founding.

To prevent CEO-itis, a CEO should regularly, once every several years, be comprehensively reviewed with an eye to detecting early signs of CEO-itis. If trouble does seem to be impending and replacement is deemed to be the appropriate remedy, don't neglect to change the systems, practices, policies, and people who have contributed to the development of CEO-itis. If you must completely replace the senior management team and the board of directors, so be it.

ACTION ITEM 4

Replace inflexible CEOs and their teams and boards that allow irreverent and capricious CEO behavior.

Building a company that can generate substantial wealth over a long period is not an easy or, at times, a pleasant task. When individuals, including CEOs, and policies—including growth-at-any-cost—conflict with the flexibility and adaptability necessary for sustainable profits, then the offending elements have to be fixed.

The good news is, when you remove these roadblocks to success, your enterprise is in a better position to deal with almost anything the future can throw at you.

ACTION ITEMS

ACTION ITEM 1
Focus on being the most adaptable business, not the biggest.

ACTION ITEM 2
Make sure the CEO knows what's going on and, if necessary, document your information in writing to the CEO.

ACTION ITEM 3
When formerly successful tactics no longer produce the expected results, listen to those people closest to the action.

ACTION ITEM 4
Replace inflexible CEOs and their teams and boards that allow irreverent and capricious behavior.

CHAPTER 9

Managing Risk

In a prior chapter I mentioned the story of how the early expansion of Olan Mills, Inc., nearly collapsed the company. Attempting to sell photography sessions in Greenville, Alabama, proved so difficult that not a single sale was logged during the first week. Disheartened and disbelieving, the sales team gave up and decided to return to Tuscaloosa and lick their wounds.

At that point, most leaders would have waved the white flag in surrender, perhaps never again to venture beyond the company's original market. Not Olan Mills, however. He knew that to continue growing, the company must expand into new areas. Having counted on sales to pay for expenses, he was confronted with no money to pay either the sales team or for their room and board. His solution: he gave the possessions of the employees, including his own, as collateral against the week's charges, promising to pay the following week. This strong-arm tactic convinced the sales team to make another effort.

Calculating that he had as much at stake as the Olan Mills, Inc., team, the rooming house proprietor purchased the first portrait plan from my grandfather. Using this as evidence of the enormous opportunity, Olan implored his team to walk faster through the community and talk to the people about portraits. Eventually, the sales team turned this small community into Olan Mills, Inc.'s, first successful model for expansion, a harbinger of many more to come.

Olan Mills, Inc., was a risk taker, from his snappy hat to his elegant shoes. When he first took the sales team to Greenville, knowing he couldn't pay for the rooming charges, he was taking a risk. If things didn't work out, he might sully the name of Olan Mills, Inc., forever. If things did work out, the effect could be the company's first successful expansion. Precisely how he calculated his odds of success we'll never know. Certainly, Olan Mills, Inc., was a skilled odds maker, experienced at assessing risk. In addition, he was an intuitive salesperson, adept when it came to predicting— within some latitude—how and when a sale could be made. Likewise, he had remarkable leadership ability, knowing to a high degree of accuracy whether people would follow his lead.

Clearly, Olan Mills, Inc., recognized the risk inherent in this move, communicated it effectively to his sales team (at least on the second trip), and did what he could to mitigate or manage the risk. The skill of dealing with risk is of paramount importance in building companies with sustainable profit potential. If you are to lead an enterprise over the long period required to build wealth, you must be able to manage risk effectively. Inadequate risk-coping will defeat excellent leadership, marketing, financial, and organizational abilities.

Surprisingly, despite the importance of risk taking, it is poorly understood in business. I am constantly confounded when talking to or hearing about entrepreneurs who, when asked who will need the product or service of their startup, "Why, everybody." In fact, of course, no product or service is in universal demand. Every product has its market, a niche that is necessarily smaller than the market as a whole. This principle is fundamental, as is the understanding that substantial risk exists that the market for any proposed product will turn out to be smaller than anticipated.

Also fundamental is the realization that, no matter how hot the demand for your product or service, you will inevitably face competition. The presence of competition presents a risk that customers may prefer a rival's products, pricing, or service to your own. Yet I often hear entrepreneurs say, "We really don't have any competition." To compound the gravity of the situation, very often these same entrepreneurs say they have no competitors and also claim that everybody needs their product or service. The likelihood of both being true, or even one, is wishful thinking.

The reality of business is that risk always exists in one form or another. One of the keys to building a lasting, wealth-generating enterprise is to recognize, manage, and communicate it to your stakeholders.

ACTION ITEM 1

Before you make any business decision, have an understanding of the major risks involved.

UNDERSTANDING RISK

Risk is also a venerable board game of the same name, played with cards and wooden markers by players attempting to take over the world. Likewise, risk is chance, an element of uncertainty, the possibility of losing everything. And risk is more. It's a verb meaning to take a flyer, to place a bet, to gamble.

Of all these meanings, however, none is quite right when it comes to the concept of risk in the business world, where it has two faces. In that context, risk is, in addition to the possibility of losing value or market share or some other worthy commodity, the chance of gaining. A risky investment or a risky move is one that, while it may show a high possibility of not working out, also shows a high possibility of returning a handsome amount. So risk is both good, and bad.

There are many different types of risk. Insurance companies cover actuarial risk, when they accept a premium in return for a promise to pay a much larger amount in the event of premature death. Financial traders run currency exchange risk when they take payment in one kind of money that will have to be converted into another kind of money, possibly losing or gaining on the exchange. Inflation risk, interest rate risk, and political risk are risks that companies run when they set prices, borrow or lend money, or enter a new governmental or regulatory arena. You run credit or repayment risk when you lend money, and lenders run this risk when they lend to you.

Virtually every move you make as a business leader incurs risk. This is not necessarily bad, for higher risk nearly always involves the possibility of higher return. A 100 percent risk-averse business leader is a 100 percent unsuccessful business leader.

In some situations, risk is held to be essentially zero, for example the risk of the U.S. government failing to pay its debts. U.S. Treasury obligations are commonly viewed as risk-free, but that assessment is only in comparison with the risks presented by other investments. While Washington, D.C., is unlikely to renege on its debts, the risk exists. You need only look at the experiences of other countries over the years, and the level of risk goes up from there.

When you accept the certainty that some measure of risk always exists, you have made a major step in managing it. Many, perhaps most, people do not see the risk inherent in their decisions. That kind of unseen risk is the killer. Just think about the countless confident predictions that have fallen prey to unforeseen risks. In 1929, for instance, the U.S. Department of Labor foresaw that, "1930 will be a splendid employment year." At the end of the 19th century, a noted American journalist predicted, "Law will be simplified over the next century. Lawyers will be diminished, and their fees will have been vastly curtailed."

OUT OF FOCUS

Robert Uihlein

In 1950, Schlitz was the largest American brewer and as late as 1973 commanded 15 percent of the U.S. market for malt beverages. With sales growing at 3 percent a year, the brewery promised to pass industry leader Anheuser-Busch and once again become king of the American brewers. In addition to a storied past, the company had a reputation for innovation, including the 1963 introduction of the flip-top lid on its canned products. It was also a significantly lower cost producer than the maker of Budweiser. Following a series of unsuccessful investments by then-CEO Robert Uihlein, including one in a duck food producer who was seen as a purchaser of the spent proceeds of Schlitz's brewing process, the company became desperate to do something to unseat Anheuser.

Matters came to a head in 1976, when the Food and Drug Administration appeared likely to implement labeling requirements that would force Schlitz to list its products's ingredients on their containers. Uihlein feared that Schlitz's cheaper ingredients would be revealed, giving Anheuser an edge. He decided to get rid of one ingredient—an unappetizing-sounding silica gel used to prolong shelf life—by adding to the beer an enzyme. The enzyme was supposed to accomplish the same thing but could be removed from the beer before shipping, meaning it would not have to be listed as an ingredient. The move was seen as a way to reduce the risk of a labeling fiasco. Because no one would see the enzyme among the ingredients, no one would be put off by it.

As it turned out, the risk was enormous. The enzyme had a reaction with other ingredients in the beer that turned it milky and cloudy after it was shipped to retailers. Beer drinkers refused to touch it. Schlitz wound up recalling more than ten million bottles and cans. More lasting damage was done to relationships with consumers and distributors. An executive shakeup took place, and the next year the company lost 10 percent of its market share, dropping to third. Uihlein didn't live to see it, having died toward the end of 1976. It's just as well, because a few years later Schlitz was acquired by another company and disappeared, a surprising end to a strategy that was supposed to reduce risk.

All leaders should understand the simple yet very profound concept of the Loser's Game, a strategy that minimizes big mistakes, and values consistent and steady performance. I picked up the game of tennis in my early 30s, and although I never really considered myself a good player, I often won matches with players far more talented and, certainly, graceful than I. I never really cared how I looked to others as I sprinted around the court chasing down shots. I found that my strategy worked. My opponents, while trying to make winning shots, would almost certainly hit the ball out of bounds or into the net—if you aim for the lines you are going to hit a few out. Their mistakes were the reason I won.

Of course this strategy would completely fail when I played against someone capable of making winning shots. In those matches I felt like a fish out of water, flailing around with a stick in my hand trying to hit missiles rocketing past.

Business leadership requires some aiming for the lines. Some of the decision risks will be rewarded, some will not. A decision that ends up costing the company a 20 percent drop requires a 25 percent pick-up for recovery. Deciding not to move forward with an ill-defined risk, or to pull out of a situation that is becoming riskier, is very often the absolute right move and an indication of a successful leader.

Why are obvious risks often not seen? Sometimes because they threaten the person doing the assessing. Consider the railroad executives who saw no risk that airlines would threaten their people-moving franchise. Other times, the risks are not seen because the leaders, while willing, are simply ignorant of risk factors. Information technology is rife with examples of this type of failure to grasp risk.

While I criticize those who fail to deal well with risk, I don't mean to suggest that dealing with risk is easy. Sometimes the perception of risk itself can affect its level. Think of the Y2K disaster. The perception of a risk of widespread computer software failures caused companies to focus huge quantities of resources on correcting error-ridden code. What happened? The disaster was averted.

Another complication lies in the fact that different risks are appropriate for different organizations. A start-up can and should take bigger risks than an established company. It faces less downside because it has less to lose.

PORTRAIT OF SUCCESS

Fred Smith

Fred Smith took many risks along the way to founding Federal Express Corp. and turning it into the $20 billion leader in express package delivery. One of the first was disbelieving the Yale University management professor who, when presented with Smith's paper describing a reliable overnight delivery service, said, "The concept is interesting and well formed, but in order to earn better than a C, the idea must be feasible." Smith founded FedEx in Little Rock, Arkansas, in 1971 and delivered the first package in 1973.

You could say that even the idea of guaranteeing overnight delivery of packages was a risk—and you'd be right. But risk was bred into FedEx culture from day one. One early employee reportedly chartered a jet to deliver a wedding dress that otherwise would have shown up after the ceremony, gambling that generating a customer service legend would outweigh the otherwise ruinous expense.

Perhaps Smith's most famous gamble occurred in the first few years of the company's existence. FedEx was in a cash bind. So serious was the shortage, that Smith would be unable to make the next payroll, coming in just a few days's time. His efforts to raise additional working capital were unsuccessful, so he took an amazing risk. Returning through Las Vegas from a trip, he went to the gambling tables and placed bets with his remaining cash. The gaming business, of course, is based on the fact that the odds always slightly favor the casinos. Given that, Smith's gamble was a likely loser.

As it happened, however, he was a winner, pocketing a reported $20,000 from his wagers. The money was enough to make the next payday, and today FedEx has more than 215,000 employees, none of them at serious risk of having their next paycheck returned stamped "Insufficient Funds."

Risk always involves the uncertainty of a result. Sometimes there's no risk at all, because you're guaranteed to fail. An example of this kind of risk is placing your hand close to the lit burner of a gas stove, or, perhaps, committing your company to financial deceit. No uncertainty exists. You will lose. The importance of avoiding these types of lose-lose scenarios is so basic, perhaps it doesn't require reinforcement. But one must understand that risk—in the sense of a chance for either positive or negative results—always exists.

ACTION ITEM 2

Only consider accepting those risks that your company/division/ department can bear in a crisis.

In 1989, the pesticide used by apple growers was said to cause cancer in children who ate treated fruit or drank the juice. The information panicked countless parents before the American Cancer Society and top medical researchers weighed in with the truth: while unrealistically extreme concentrations would indeed cause tumors, Alar was in reality less dangerous than many naturally occurring substances. The scare cost apple growers hundreds of millions of dollars but had the positive result of contributing to a less hysterical climate in reporting potential health risks. Regulatory agencies, and to a large extent the media, learned that communicating the nature and level of risks is both very important and not that simple.

Another, more recent example of the importance of communicating risk is drawn from the Enron debacle of 2001. The Houston company evolved over a decade or so from a staid natural gas producer into a high-flying trader of contracts for energy delivery and other more exotic commodities such as telecommunications bandwidth. In the process, it grew to become the fifth-largest company on the *Fortune* 500 list. Its president, Jeffrey Skilling, was regarded nearly as a magician, able to contrive incredible revenues and profits out of an industry that few could even imagine existing. The market valued the company at more than $66 billion at various points.

In 2001, the whole thing came tumbling down. Skilling resigned in August, a move never explained adequately by remaining company management. The company's reporting of arcane accounting creations called *special purpose entities* was suspected of being used to hide debts off the balance sheet. In an amazingly short period, the true risk behind Enron's house of cards was revealed, and the shares tumbled to trade below 50 cents—from a high of over $80 dollars.

The basic failure here is the failure to communicate risk to Enron's investors, to stock analysts, and possibly to the company's chairman and board of directors. Rather than serving as a tool for information, the annual reports and required filings were used to obscure Enron's true financial condition. The proper way to communicate risk is, of course, far different.

COMMUNICATING RISKS

When communicating risk factors, start by considering your audience very carefully. You must frame the risk you perceive in terms that the audience can understand. Talking over the heads of your audience increases confusion and therefore questions. Take into account biases and desires as well. For instance, Enron emitted hints that financial problems existed well before the collapse. But analysts and investors, entranced by the company's phenomenal growth and their own equally impressive gains on its shares, were not disposed to listen. Similarly, in the wake of the failure, it became plain that some of the financial transactions in which it engaged were too complex for its board of directors to properly grasp the risk they carried. If your audience can't, or won't, understand you easily, you'll have to make an extra effort to convey risk.

Because of the potential for problems, only one time is right for communicating risk: as early as possible. Efforts to communicate risk to stakeholders should be an integral part of risk assessment and management activities. As soon as you identify a risk, tell the people who need to know about it.

The only delay you might consider would be because of the public impact of your announcement. For instance, if the Alar critics had delayed their press conferences and news releases until they had checked with mainstream health authorities, they might never have released their damaging inaccuracies. They also might have held back if they had anticipated how their pronouncements would be received.

Assessing the public response is itself risky. There is always the "fright factor." People just find some things scary. Whether and to what extent a risk advisory should be made is often governed by the means selected. The company grapevine can be effective in some cases, but it is more likely to spread inaccuracies and compel a hasty formal release. The news media and other formal information transmission channels are preferred choices. Managing the message is crucial. If the news you have is either quite scary (We may shut down two plants.) or likely to be widely and rapidly disseminated, perhaps beyond your ability to control it, you have to take extra care in how and when you announce it.

On the other hand, nonscary risks that people are unlikely to discuss may require an extra push to be effectively communicated. You can give a risk advisory extra emphasis by targeting your warnings to key stakeholders such as influential department heads. Also, take into consideration how those key individual audiences will react to the news.

Before you say anything about a risk, you have to know why you want to communicate it and must have agreement concerning the risk from your top advisors. Prioritize those aims so that you work hardest on the main goals.

When communicating risk, start with what is known and work your way to the less certain information. For instance, if you are closing an East Coast plant, begin with that. If the closing of this plant means you may be unable to serve Atlantic seaboard markets, that outcome is less certain and should be less emphasized. Make clear what issues require further investigation and how you are going about getting that information. Acknowledge the uncertainties that aren't likely to be resolved.

Anytime you communicate a risk, clarify what you are doing to deal with the risk. Make sure that the measures you describe fit what you are saying. Don't warn about the possible loss of a major customer while putting forth efforts to develop minor customers as a possible solution.

When risky information is conveyed, emotions will likely become involved, so you must take them into account. See that your emotional tone is appropriate and, if necessary, make space for others to express their emotions, which may range from anger to despair.

It is always important to express risks in comparison to baseline risks. For instance, if the risk of spending heavily to enter a new market is that you may experience a temporary decline in profits, what are the risks if you do nothing? If inactivity is likely to lead to a long-term profit slide, then the risk of entering the new market appears more palatable.

Finally, discuss what you are doing to monitor the situation. Discuss procedures to gather information, and assess progress in mitigating the risk. Show how you are open to reviewing strategy, gaining additional insight, and, if necessary, taking assistance.

ACTION ITEM 3

Communicate all significant business risks to shareholders and superiors prior to taking action.

MANAGING RISKS

"The essence of risk management," Peter Bernstein writes in his best-seller *The Remarkable Story of Risk*, "lies in maximizing the areas where we have some control over the outcome while minimizing the areas where we have absolutely no control over the outcome and the linkage between effect and cause is hidden from us."

This definition is important, because it focuses attention not on avoiding anything that is uncertain or on doing nothing, but on taking advantage of what we know, while limiting the potential damage of what we don't know.

This is actually the third part of risk management, however. A more expansive view of risk management includes the identification of potential losses and their causes, as well as an assessment of the amount of loss that may be sustained. After these two steps are complete, you may begin trying to control or limit risk.

Information is the central element in a risk management effort. You must have information about the number, type, source, and potency of risk factors before you can do much about them. This information is, unfortunately, almost always incomplete. In the case of true innovations, it is sometimes difficult to obtain more than sketchy outlines of risk factors. Bernstein compares this situation to the risk of going out with out an umbrella on a cloudy day. Most of us can tell by a look at clouds what the chances of rain are in the next few hours. But when the clouds are unlike anything we've ever seen before, we don't know when to bring the umbrella.

One way to get information is to conduct tests and pilot programs. This approach would have served Olan Mills, Inc., well when it was attempting to enter the glamour photography field. Rather than aggressively entering the field with plans to open 94 stores in a year, the company would have done better just to open a few stores. It would have gained valuable insight into the economics of operating photo studios in high-cost, extended-hours shopping malls. Diversification is one of the most accepted means to reduce risk. Scholarly studies as well as nearly a half-century of investors' experience have shown that a diversified portfolio of bonds, equities, cash, and other alternative assets will outperform a concentrated portfolio over a long period of time.

The same is true of businesses. A business that relies on a single big customer may well generate higher profit margins than a company that serves many customers, but the firm with the diverse customer base is clearly better positioned for wealth-building over the long haul. What will happen to the first company when its big customer decides to go elsewhere? Its demise will follow soon. A slower fate may await if the big customer, coming to realize its power over its supplier, squeezes pricing until margins shrink and disappear.

ACTION ITEM 4

Manage all corporate and personal risks that might materially impact shareholder value.

OUT OF FOCUS

Gene Amdahl

If ever anything looked like a sure thing, Trilogy Systems was it. Gene Amdahl, one of the pioneers of business computers and principal designer of IBM's storied System 360, the mainframe computers upon which Big Blue's prosperity was built in the 1960s and 1970s, started the company. Amdahl was named one of the "1,000 Makers of the 20th Century" by *The Times* of London, only one of many accolades he has received.

Amdahl, a South Dakota native, left IBM in 1970 to start Amdahl Corp., the first firm to manufacture plug-compatible computers, which could work with IBM's own disk drives, printers, software, and other components but would cost much less. The move was considered foolhardy, especially considering Amdahl's eminence at IBM, but he prospered enormously as an entrepreneur. In its first full year, the start-up shipped $96 million and tripled that amount in its third year. In many ways, Amdahl's success modeled the success of later PC-compatible entrepreneurs such as Bill Gates and Michael Dell.

But ten years later, the restless Amdahl left his own company to start Trilogy Systems Corp. The legendary computer entrepreneur easily raised $230 million in start-up capital. But Trilogy proved Amdahl's downfall. The company's advanced technology was promising, but an incredible series of disasters dogged it. Heavy rain slowed the building of the plant where its advanced semiconductors were to be made. Then the clean room was damaged, and many of the costly prototypes were destroyed. By then, a third of the start-up capital was spent. The development project was scuttled and the remainder of the funds used to purchase another computer company, Elxsi Corp.

Incredibly, the nearly quarter-billion in start-up funds, coupled with Amdahl's legendary innovation, was inadequate to make Trilogy a prosperous concern. It wound up becoming part of Elxsi Corp., an Orlando company that has since left the computer business and now generates a substantial portion of its revenues from manufacturing equipment for inspecting sewers—a development that would be unbelievably ironic if it were not true.

The investors who funded Trilogy could probably have benefited from one of the modern Elxsi's remote-controlled video cameras, but instead they were blinded by Gene Amdahl's reputation and Amdahl Corp.'s past financial success. They didn't stop to consider the differences between Amdahl's plug-compatible designs and the radically different technologies he was now proposing. Amdahl himself went on to start two more companies, neither of which ascended to anything like his prior ventures's prominence.

Risk takers are celebrated because they do surprising things, crafting enterprises that rise from nowhere to prominence overnight. Risk managers are ignored because they do mundane things, reducing their profits by reducing their risks while building organizations that steadily create wealth over long periods of time. That doesn't mean that risk takers are superior, that taking more risks is always a good idea, or even that selected risks that have paid off for others would be a good idea for you.

Olan Mills, Inc., sold some of his first photographs to families who didn't realize they were posing in front of a filmless camera. My grandfather didn't load the camera with film for the simple reason that, until he received the portrait subjects's down payment for their photos, he couldn't afford to buy it. The risk of being caught deceiving his customers may have been appropriate for him, in that day and in that place and with his company at that stage of development. But today, Olan Mills, Inc., could scarcely contemplate photographing people with empty cameras, cashing their checks and then calling them for another sitting on the pretext of an error in the developing process. Today's sophisticated customers wouldn't stand for it, modern deceptive advertising laws would penalize the company severely, and to cap it all, it simply doesn't make sense for any large, well-financed company take such a risk.

Different risks at different times are appropriate for different companies. Knowing your company and the risks it can absorb is one of the keys to building wealth long-term and increasing the likelihood that, someday, some future business writer will feature your company as a Portrait of Success.

ACTION ITEMS

ACTION ITEM 1
Before you make any business decision have an understanding of the major risks involved.

ACTION ITEM 2
Only consider accepting those risks that your company/division/ department can bear in a crisis.

ACTION ITEM 3
Communicate all significant business risks to shareholders and superiors prior to taking action.

ACTION ITEM 4
Manage all corporate and personal risks that might materially impact shareholder value.

CONCLUSION

Closing Reflections

During my career at Olan Mills, Inc., I spent many hours walking about the company's plants, offices, and field operations talking with employees. Very often, as I was visiting a company facility, people would approach, eager to tell me their personal stories about the early days with Olan Mills. Many of these stories were from senior employees who had worked alongside my grandfather.

A fair number of these anecdotes had to do with the style of attire my grandfather expected and, to a lesser extent, required of his employees. For example, if you were a woman working in the office, and in many cases even in a production facility, he expected to see you wearing white gloves—the type that were common to well-dressed women before the 1960s. Men wore suits, ties, and hats no matter how high the temperature in those days without air conditioning.

Out of all these stories, one uniquely sticks out as unusual and memorable. During World War II, rationing of materials such as silk and nylon meant that American women found it difficult, if not impossible, to obtain stockings. Olan Mills, however, required his female employees to maintain his dress code, and this called for them to wear stockings. To comply, or at least appear to comply, female workers applied leg makeup to give the illusion of hose. This required the skilled use of an eyebrow pencil to draw an imitation seam up the backside of each leg.

Leg makeup—now that's a management concept nobody knows about any more, and I'm certainly not trying to revive it. Leg makeup may have played a role in setting the tone and culture for Olan Mills in those early days, but it has no place today. Although requiring it no doubt made an impression on Olan Mills's employees, so much so that they remember it to this day, it's fair to say that the era of leg makeup has passed.

Portraits of Success is not about leg makeup. That may not sound like much of a claim, but if you examine the concepts presented in most management books, you will find yourself confronted with a great deal of information that amounts to the same thing—ideas that are nothing more than dressed up jargon or which might work in their time, for a time, but aren't likely be useful for long. The ideas presented here, as befits concepts intended for the building of long-term success, are timeless. They will work now; they will work in the future. There is no leg makeup here.

Even ideas that are far more current than leg makeup usually don't pass the tests that I require to adopt them within client firms. In fact, I have a positive distrust of management fashions and fads, whatever they may be. I believe—and the record bears me out—that whatever is newly recognized as powerful and cutting-edge today is very likely either on the way out or will soon be passé. You have only to think of the many companies and concepts held up as paragons only to be revealed as fallible almost before the ink was dry on the many stories that heralded them as immortal.

Most recently, Enron Corp. of Houston was revealed to have feet of clay. The company's 2001 bankruptcy filing and the subsequent accounting and other scandals came only months after it was widely regarded as a new paradigm for success: the bold creator of a new business model and originator of an entire industry built around complex financial schemes. It makes you wonder what is likely to happen to the current set of revered companies, ideas, and leaders, whoever they might be. Commonly accepted business wisdom is, in fact, rarely wise at all.

Ideas *de jour* aside, I am confident that the concepts presented in *Portraits of Success* will prove timeless. That does not mean they will always work equally well or in every case. No business system is successful in every application. Many comparisons have been made between business and mechanistic systems such as physics, computer science, engineering, and so on, attempting to equate one with the other.

The difference between physics and business is that the characters in a business scenario are intelligent. People—including your competitors—learn and respond. As a result, the environment in which you operate changes according to circumstances. The presence of intelligent, educated, constantly changing people in a system makes it impossible to accurately predict what will happen when an action is taken. That is why I don't present these ideas as a system or an algorithm with absolute and predictable results.

But the tools are here. While this approach to business success may not be paint-by-numbers, it is a complete theory. It is a set of tools and concepts that is, by itself, sufficient for building long-term business success.

The most conspicuous omission in these pages is a definition of *what success is to you,* and in many ways, that definition is the most important part of the equation. This is no trivial matter. The inability to correctly identify personal success has led to the failure of many closely held companies. In too many cases, pursuing success is like playing a football game in which the goal line retreats the closer you get to it. Too many business leaders have never answered the basic question, "What is success to me and this firm?" The most important component in that question, and the one most easily overlooked, is the fact that success, in the long-term, often has very little to do with piles of money.

To return to Enron for a moment, many people did receive a lot of money from their relationship with Enron. Countless employees, executives, suppliers, stockholders, and lenders who dealt with the company over the years came away richer. But was that success? In the way we're talking about success, no, it is not. We're talking about generational success, the kind that doesn't consist of a quick cash-out or a crash cushioned by a golden parachute.

I was reminded of the importance and value of a long-term effort, as opposed to quick fixes, when not long ago I hosted a large dinner party in our home that included a number of business colleagues. I was pleased to observe my 13-year-old son, Warren, shaking hands with each guest, looking them in the eye and saying clearly, "Hello. My name is Warren." The next day, several people asked me whether I had trained my son to behave like that. Somewhat surprised, I said, "Of course. My wife, Sarah, and I, with help from the grandparents, have been training him since he was born."

Looking back on that experience, I think what people were really asking was whether I had specifically drilled him just before the gathering got underway on how I expected him to greet people. But, of course, we didn't start on his education an hour before dinner, or even in the prior year. We're talking about training for life, and the training—if I can be excused for misusing that term—of a business is similar. You don't do it well when you try to do it in an hour. You only generate persistent success when you apply these lessons over a significant portion of a lifetime.

My emphasis on long-term success in no way reflects a dislike, disregard, or a "less than" belief should success come quickly or easily. I admire the accomplishments of successful people and desire success, of virtually every ilk, in my own life and in that of my clients. From my experience, however, success should not be confused with mere survival. I don't encourage people or firms merely to get by. Increasing revenue and market share isn't the only means for measuring long-term prosperity. You should also constantly expand your abilities, your commitment, and your openness to learning and adapting.

If business were a marriage, which for some it is, would you want to look back at your 50th anniversary and say, "That was okay," or, if you managed and led with long view objectives guiding your decisions, might you look back and instead say, "That was fantastic!"

These ideas apply to any company, but no one company will embody all of them. While I have discussed many companies in this book, you don't see me holding any single firm up as a paragon, a perfect avatar of the *Portraits of Success* keys to long-term business success. That includes Olan Mills, Inc., both now and during my tenure there.

The reason I don't have such an example is because there isn't one. *Portraits of Success* comes from the best practices of many, many clients. Is it easy to hew to this theoretical ideal? No, it's not. Is it expected? Certainly not. Would you be better off if you applied most of them? Absolutely!

Another point relates to the portraits of the many companies, both successful and unsuccessful, to which you have now been exposed. Although I tell stories about how other people apply the Keys and develop their own portraits, this is not intended to be a book about how others do it. It's about how you can change your company, and your life. That's a portrait that only you can develop.

My last story doesn't have anything to do with the sustainability of a company. It has to do with passing, and putting life into perspective. It has nothing directly to do with business. It's about family, my family. When I was in second grade, my 14-month-old brother, Travis, drowned in our backyard pool. I was the one who found Travis in the water. No one was at fault, according to the standards of the time, which didn't require or expect people to enclose their pools in toddler-proof fences. Travis opened a sliding glass door and managed to get outside without anyone noticing. Then he just walked into the pool.

This was a life-altering event for me, and as a consequence, I believe I have always been able to keep business and family in proper perspective. I saw firsthand the anguish of my parents and have lived since that day with the knowledge that I would never know the brother I once had. Both at Olan Mills, Inc., and in my consulting business, I believe I have seen it all when it comes to closely held companies. The one recurring theme I see in those that are dysfunctional and headed toward gloom and doom is the inability of the key leadership to put and keep business interests in their proper place.

Hopefully, this story will emphasize that winning in business by securing that key account or achieving a record profit doesn't seem very important in the overall context of your life needs—and it isn't.

You need to keep this in mind as you go about building the kind of long-term success that will be around for the people who come after you. Just because nobody else builds fences around their pools doesn't mean it's a bad idea, should the idea first occur to you. That's the kind of long-term risk management and creative thinking that pays off. Although it may seem more urgent to spend another hour at the office than to spend time with your family, that doesn't mean it's a good idea.

Successful, long-lived, wealth-producing businesses are more like living entities than machines. If we treat them as if that's what they are, requiring a broad panoply of nutrients, we will have a better chance of producing the genuine, enduring variety. And, in one of those powerful paradoxes, I believe that when you come to realize that business isn't the only important thing in your life, you have a better chance of being a very good, and highly successful, business leader. When it comes to what really matters in life, very often you must give a little to gain a lot. Putting your business interests in perspective, that is living your life in proper balance by giving *less* to the company rather than *more* is nearly always the road to greater financial success and is always the path to greater personal fulfillment. It assures you will be more grounded in life, so that when one of those ugly curves comes your way, you won't become unseated.

This has been a wide-ranging chapter, venturing from leg make-up to untimely death. I would like to be able to close by telling you what became of that company founded by my grandfather and represented by that gilt signature on so many millions of family portraits—but I can't. That story doesn't have an ending. Olan Mills, Inc., like so many companies today, is confronting profound changes in markets, technologies, and trends. How well it negotiates them will determine whether it retains its place among those firms that experience sustainable success.

Meanwhile, the image it provides does endure. The next time you examine photos of the ones you love, check for that Olan Mills signature. Let it be a reminder that the goal of your business leadership is to create an enterprise that flourishes and endures, just like your feelings for the people in those photographs.

INDEX

A

Acceptance stage, 191
Accountability, 36, 69–70, 80
Action
  balance, 162–63
  business leadership, 46–47
  common direction, 100–101
  communication, 132–33
  meritocracy, 63–64
  next generation leaders, 80
  risk management, 214
  survival, 198
  traditions/myths/ shared beliefs, 182–83
Actuarial risk, 202
Adaptability, 18, 185–86, 198
Advancement
  preparation, 61, 64

Amdahl, Gene, 212–13
American Airlines, 11–12
Anger stage, 191
Annual meetings, 120
Attitude, 25–26
Attributes, 28
Avery, Sewell, 196

B

Balance, 6, 220–21
  business life, 154, 155, 163
  changes and, 153
  family life, 155, 163
  health, 155–56
  importance of, 152–53
  indicators, 159–62
  passion and, 147–52
  self, 158
  social life, 157–58
  spiritual, 156–57
Ballmer, Steve, 17
Behavioral actions, 191–92
Berkshire Hathaway, 115–16

Bernstein, Peter, 210, 211
Bonus, 56
Boomeranging, 65–66
Bottom-to-top
  communication, 105–6
Boyle, Gertrude, 143–44, 146, 147
Boyle, Tim, 144
Branson, Richard, 138
Buffett, Warren, 115–16
Burnett, Samuel Burk, 172
Business
  failure, 9–10
  life, 154, 155, 163
  mores, 62–63, 64
  success, 8–9
  transformation, 144

C

Candor, 97, 124–25, 133
Canion, Rod, 100
Capital, lack of, 10–12
Career exploration, 41–42, 147
CEO-itis, 193–98

Chain of command,
120–24, 133
Change
    balance and, 153
    barriers, 187–89
    management, 187–90
    motivational forces,
        189–90
    stages of, 190–92
Charisma, 138
Chevron Texaco
    Corporation, 53
Choices, 40–42, 46–47, 79
Civil Rights Act of 1964,
    50, 51
Clark, Jim, 135
ClubCorp, Inc., 73–74
Code of Conduct, 108–9
Cognitive behavioral
    therapy, 27
Collaboration, 70–71, 80
Columbia Sportswear
    Co., 144
Common direction
    benefits of, 88–90
    feedback, 95
    finding, 81–83,
        91–101
    as guide, 98, 101
    information
        provisions, 94–99
    lack of, 84–86
    management and,
        88–89
    methods, 93–94
    need for, 15–16
Communication
    of bad news, 110,
        128–30, 133
    chain of command
        and, 120–24
    challenges, 104–6
    of common direction,
        94–95, 96, 100
    control of, 111–12
    face-to-face, 114–15,
        117
    failures, 102–3
    goal, 107, 112

in hostile
    environment, 123
importance of, 16
leadership and,
    106–7, 132
limits, 110–12
parties involved, 103
policies, 109, 132
of power distribution,
    122–23
priority of, 114–15,
    133
of risk, 206–10, 214
semantic mismatch,
    105
survey, 112–14
traits, 104–12
triangular, 104–5
two-way, 108, 109,
    126–30, 132
written messages,
    109, 133
Compaq Computer
    Corp., 99–100, 178
Compensation
    excessive, 34–35, 46
    issues, 56
    performance-based,
        32–33, 46
    results-oriented,
        55–57, 63
    rule, 56
Competence, 25, 26
Competition, 92
Competitive edge, 8
Concept failure, 9
Confusion, 106
Contradictory initiatives,
    106
Contribution, 7
Control issues, 85
Cooper Clinic, 156
Coordination, 103
Corporate purpose,
    92–94, 101
Corporate stories
    creation of, 171–72,
        175, 182
    importance of, 167–68

message, 164–65
tradition-building,
    176, 182
Corrective action, 98
Creativity, 138
Credibility, 94
Credit risk, 202
Currency exchange risk,
    202
Customer meetings, 118,
    119
Customer service, 90–91,
    145, 146, 167

D

Dallas Cowboys, 88
Dedman, Jr., Robert,
    73–74
Dell, Michael, 99–100,
    138, 170
Dell Computer
    Corporation, 99–100,
    170
Denial stage, 191
Denny's, 54
Digital Equipment Corp.,
    100
Disagreements, 97–98
Discrimination lawsuits,
    53
Disney, Roy, 23
Diversification, 211
Diversity, 52–53, 61, 64
Drucker, Peter, 112, 124
Dunlap, Al, 29, 192–93

E

Educational background,
    50
Employee
    confusion, 106
    growth, 14–15
    meetings, 118, 119
    morale, 32–33
    sharing of, 70–71, 80
Employment
    agreements, 147
    discrimination in,
        50–51, 52

family policy, 79–80
Enron Corp., 184, 207,
    208, 216–17, 218
Entitlement attitude, 28,
    33
Ethics, 93–94
Ethnicity, 50–51
Excellence, 144
Experiences, 73, 75–76,
    80

F
Failure
    learning through, 36,
        46
    reasons for, 9–10
Family council, 117–18
Family life, 155, 163
Favoritism, 49–51
Fear, 188
Federal Radio Act of
    1912, 103
FedEx, 205–6
Feedback
    common direction
        and, 95
    criteria for, 47
    leadership and, 41–43
    360-degree, 125–26
Financial details, 95–96
Financial success, 142–43
Fiorina, Carly, 178
Flexibility, 8, 53
Ford, Henry, 97
Ford, Jr., William Clay, 48
Ford Motor Co., 49–50
Forgiveness, 77–78, 80
Founders' offspring, 141
Four Sixes Ranch, 172
Fright factor, 208–9
Fun, 6

G
Gates, Bill, 135, 138
Gender discrimination,
    51, 141
General Electric Co., 55,
    70, 91, 189
General Motors, 188

Gerstner, Jr., Louis V., 83
Getty, J. Paul, 148–50
Getty Oil Company, 148
Gilchrist, Henry, 110
Glass ceiling concept, 51
Goals, 5
Go-between, 104–5
Golden handcuffs, 147
Good Old Boy Club
    (GOB), 53–55, 63
Grapevine, 111–12
Green organizations, 93
Growth, 8–9, 14–15

H
Haggar III, Joe M.,
    139–40
Haggar Apparel Co.,
    139–40
Harley Davidson, 145
Hefner, Christie, 23
Hewlett-Packard Co.,
    100, 178
High performers, 62–63
Hostile environment, 123
Humanity, 2
Human resource
    management, 2–3
Hunt, Johnnie, 45
Huntsman, Joe, 159–61

I
Image, 89–90, 100, 101,
    142
Incentive, 56
Individual success, 4–7
Inflation risk, 202
Information
    risk management
        and, 211
    sharing of, 94–99, 123
Innovation, 138
Insight, 73
Integrity, 26
Intellectual capital, 15
Interest rate risk, 202
Internal conflict, 85
International Business
    Machines Corp., 83

International Garment
    Processors, 140, 143
Isolation, 195

J
J.B. Hunt Transport, 45
Jenkens & Gilchrist, 110

K
Katz, Barry, 79
Katz, Marc, 78–79
Katz's Deli and Bar,
    78–79
Kelleher, Herbert, 165–66
Kimberly-Clark, 192
King, Alice, 141
King, Richard, 141, 143
King, Rollin, 165
King Ranch, 141, 143
Kleberg, Robert, 141
Kleberg, Sally, 141

L
Latch Apparel Company,
    135, 136
Leadership
    abdicating, 86
    accountability, 36
    communication and,
        106–7, 132
    direction from, 85–86
    experience, 38–40
    grooming successors,
        13
    lack of, 132
    low self-esteem in,
        34–36, 46
    narcissism in, 28–29,
        33–34
    nepotism in, 29–32
    next generation,
        21–23, 33–34, 46,
        65–80
    performance-based,
        32–33, 46
    rehiring policies and,
        65–67
    self-esteem and, 13,
        21–25

Leadership *continued*
  specialization and,
    71–73
  stair-step approach,
    39–40
Learning organization,
  78
Legend Airlines, 11–12
Legends, 18
Lever-Pollary, Teresa,
  169, 175
Levi Strauss Company,
  143
Lifestyle
  balance, 153–62
  changes, 153
  multidimensional,
    152
Lincoln, Abraham, 45
Listening skill, 196
Living consciously, 26
Living purposely, 26
Long-term perspective,
  1–2
Loser's game strategy,
  204
Loyalty, 79
Lutz, Bob, 188

M

Management failure, 10
Market share, 15, 91
Mars, 8
Meeting, 118–20, 133
Mentor, 44–45, 47
Meritocracy
  creation of, 13–14,
    48–49, 53–64
  failure risks, 51–53
  ignoring, 49–51
  nepotism and, 49–50
Methods, 93–94
Microsoft, 17
Miller, E.L., 147
Mills, Olan, 16
Mills II, Olan, 138
Mistakes, 75–77, 78
Montgomery Ward, 18,
  184, 196

Morale, 138
Munger, Charlie, 116
Myths, 17–18, 167–73

N

Narcissism, 27–29, 33–34,
  44
Nasser, Jacques, 48
Nepotism, 29–32
Netpliance, 84–85
Netscape, 135
Newell Farms, 130–31
Nightime Pediatric
  Clinics, 169
Nike, 144
Nordstrom, 167

O

Objective feedback,
  125–26
Occam's Razor, 2
Olan Mills
  chain of command,
    121
  common direction, 15
  continuity program,
    82
  corporate stories,
    164–65, 175, 215–16
  customer service, 90,
    146
  leadership, 39–40
  risk management,
    199–200
  telemarketing
    program, 82, 98
  traditions/myths,
    17–18
Open book management,
  123–24
Open door policies, 95
Organization chart, 122
Overspecialization, 71, 72
Ownership, 122, 128

P

Pan American, 18, 184
Passion
  balance and, 147–52

beyond, 142
  cultivation of, 16–17
  existence of, 139
  leadership and,
    134–48
Performance
  appraisal, 55–57
  evaluation, 58
  improvement, 127
Performance-based
  promotion, 32–33, 46,
    57–59, 63
Perks, 147, 162
Personal happiness, 6, 25,
  26
Personal integrity, 26
Peter Principle, 58
Planning failure, 10
Playboy Enterprises, 23
Political risk, 202
Power distribution,
  122–23
Professional effort,
  151–52
Profitability, 8
Proteges, 44–45
Protocols, 62–63, 64
Public response, 208–9
Pullman, 18, 184

Q

Quinn, Fergal, 146, 174

R

Recruitment issues,
  51–52, 61
Rehiring policies, 65–67
Repayment risk, 202
Respect, 32–33, 145
Risk
  communication of,
    206–10, 214
  management, 18,
    199–201, 210–14
  reduction, 211
  takers, 77–78, 80, 213
  types of, 202
  understanding, 201–8
Rodman, Dennis, 59–61

S

Schedule, 154
Schlitz, 203–4
Scott Paper, 192
Sears & Roebuck, 18, 184
Self-acceptance, 26
Self-assertiveness, 26
Self care, 158, 163
Self-esteem, 7
   accountability and, 36
   ancient roots, 27–28
   appropriate levels,
     44–45
   attitude towards, 45
   building, 38–42,
     46–47
   components, 25–26
   definition of, 25
   development of,
     26–27
   leadership and, 12, 13,
     21–25
   narcissism and,
     28–29, 44
   nepotism and, 29–32
   power dynamics and,
     31
   psychological
     problems and, 24
   signs of low, 34–36
   value of, 23
Self-responsibility, 26
Self-worth, 25, 26, 27
Semantic mismatch, 105
Shared beliefs
   building, 17–18,
     177–81, 182–83
   importance of,
     166–67, 182
Silicon Graphics, 135
Skilling, Jeffrey, 207
Smith, Fred, 205–6
Snecma, 70
Social life, 157–58, 163

Southwest Airlines,
   165–66
Specialization, 71–73
Spiritual life, 156–57, 163
Squibb, Randy, 126
Stakeholders, 117
Start-up companies, 138
Steinbrenner, George,
   86–88
Stora Enso Oyj, 185–86
Storying around
   technique, 181
Strategic alliances, 70
Strategy, 19–20
Strengths/weaknesses,
   96–97
Success
   definition of, 3–4,
     217–18
   keys to, 12–20
Sunbeam, 29, 192–93
Survey, 112–14, 113
Survival, 18

T

Tandem, 100
Testing, 84
360-degree feedback,
   125–26
Tilton, Carr, 68–69
Timeframe, 94
Timing, 119–20
TippingPoint
   Technologies, Inc.,
   84–85, 188
Titles, 122–23
Traditions, 17–18,
   167–68, 174–77, 182
Training, 218
Transformation, 144, 162
Transparent
   management, 123–24
Triangular
   communication, 104–5
Trilogy Systems Corp.,
   212–13

Trump, Donald, 28–29
Two-way
   communication, 108,
   109, 126–30, 132

U

Uihlein, Robert, 203–4

V

Validation, 112–13
Values, 166–67
Viramontes, Cesar, 140,
   141
Viramontes, Heidi, 140,
   141, 143

W

Wackenhut, Richard R.,
   37–38
Walk around technique,
   95
Wal-Mart, 88
Walt Disney Co., 23
Walton, Sam, 88, 145
Wealth building, 7, 143
Wealth preservation, 143
Welch, Jack, 55, 70, 91,
   135
Whitetail, Inc., 68–69
Williamson, Philip, 136,
   139
Williamson-Dickie
   Manufacturing Co.,
   135–37
Wright Amendment, 11,
   12
Written messages, 109,
   132

X

Xerox, 18, 184

Y

Yankees, 87–88

Portraits of Success

An ideal read for every member of a family, or closely held, business. For quantities of *Portraits of Success*, please contact Terri Joseph in Special Sales, 800-621-9621, ext. 4307, or tjoseph@dearborn.com. You may also order this book with a customized cover featuring your company name, logo, and message.

3220